Uncove...g ...y......gy
The Complete Collection
(5 Books in 1)

The Last Beginner's Guide On Norse Mythology, Celtic Mythology, Egyptian Mythology ,Japanese Mythology and Greek Mythology with 2 epic bonus

Harris Thompson

TABLE OF CONTENTS

Introduction

What is Mythology and Why it Fascinates Us

Mythology! Just the word conjures up an array of gods and goddesses, heroes and monsters, timeless legends and timeless tales spanning millennia. But before diving deeper into its depths, let us pause to consider exactly what mythology entails: At its core, mythology refers to an intricate system of tales or legends held sacred by various cultures over time - serving as cultural lexicon that communicates beliefs, values, fears and aspirations from within their communities.

It captivates us all; with tales that draw us out of the ordinary world and into one where anything seems possible; where mortals converse with gods, defeat fearsome monsters, and even outwit death itself. Think about it: Haven't you ever wished for Herculean strength or Athena-esque wisdom? These stories capture our imagination precisely because they open doors into worlds we could only dream of otherwise.

But mythology serves a much greater purpose than entertainment alone: It serves as an ancient educational tool filled with life lessons, philosophical inquiries, and ethical dilemmas. Tales of hubris warn against arrogance while sacrifice inspires us to become better people. From ancient Egyptian morality tales to Greek philosophical quandaries these tales allow us to grapple with life and its mysteries.

Never let us forget how deeply mythology pervades our daily lives; from fascination with the zodiac to planet names derived from Roman deities. All these threads make up part of an intricate tapestry that continues to develop, adapt, and expand today.

As we embark on this enthralling voyage through mythological terrains, let us keep this in mind: We're not simply recreating old tales; rather we are participating in an ageless tradition which continues to shape how we view the world and ourselves within it.

Understanding Myth in Culture

So what role does myth play in our societies? First off, myths act like DNA for societies by codifying ideals, customs, and even collective memory into stories and characters that form part of its fabric. Just like you couldn't take away a strand of DNA without disrupting cell function and losing its identity altogether, taking out mythology would mean taking out part of its cultural identity with it.

Myths are more than bedtime stories for adults; they serve as our society's roadmap, guiding us through milestones. Think about your coming-of-age ceremony or New Year celebration: chances are, myths from your culture have had some influence. From baby-naming ceremonies in various African cultures (inspired by ancient oral traditions) to Japan's Shichi-Go-San festival which acts as a rite of passage for young children (Shichi-Go-San festival), myths play an essential role in life from beginning to grave.

Myths serve a dual function. On one hand, they're great story-tellers that offer entertaining tales while on the other they provide social bonds to bring people together - be it at a campfire, theater performance or online-- when we share myths we're doing more than simply passing time: we're building community, belonging and shared values - this is especially critical in today's increasingly fragmented and dispersed society.

Myths have the power to shape political landscapes and history events. Have you heard of 'Manifest Destiny,' which guided American westward expansion? This concept rests heavily on mythological beliefs such as divine providence and national exceptionalism that provide justification for wars and influence laws on a national scale. Myths can validate authority, justify wars, and even alter laws of the land itself.

As we explore Greek epics, Celtic lore, or Egyptian afterlife mythology, let's keep this in mind: each myth we come across serves to uphold its respective civilization and provide its foundational structure. These tales aren't simply entertaining stories; they form culture over time.

How to Navigate This Book

Let's get down to business! Now that you have this hefty tome of epic tales and in-depth mythological studies in your hands, you may be asking "Where should I begin?" Relax-- this book is designed as your gateway into Greek, Norse, Celtic, Egyptian and Japanese mythologies as well as bonuses! Whether this is your inaugural journey into mythological realms or you are an expert mythological traveler seeking your next journey-we have you covered!

As you'll notice, the book is divided into four main areas that focus on different cultural mythologies. Each area is further subdivided into three chapters that explore its myths, characters and themes specific to that culture. But don't feel limited by having to read each section sequentially! Feel free to explore Loki before Aphrodite; think of this book like a buffet of myths; sampling everything or diving deeply into those that interest you most is all within its pages!

Now are you ready? Whether you plan on reading this book from beginning to end or skimming the pages at will, remember that there is no right or wrong way of discovering these age-old tales. Every myth contributes to human culture and imagination and you'll come away not only with an in-depth knowledge of myths from around the globe but also an appreciation for how they continue to influence and enrich our daily lives.

Book 1: Greek Mythology

1.1 The Greek Pantheon: Beyond Zeus and Hera

Now is the time to take an in-depth look at Greek mythology's pantheon--including Olympian gods and goddesses, deities, divine entities beyond Mount Olympus, as well as other divine entities residing outside its realms. While Zeus and Hera might be best known, Greek mythology offers a host of characters with distinct quirks, powers, and captivating tales such as Athena emerging fully armed from Zeus after Zeus swallowed Metis' pregnant mother Metis whole; or Dionysus the god of wine also known for both inducing ecstasy while unleashing chaos when representing its vintages he represents!

Let us also give a shout-out to the minor deities and divine spirits--including nymphs, satyrs, and centaurs--that add another layer of richness to this already vibrant tapestry. It is essential to recognize that the Greek pantheon is not an autonomous entity; rather it was closely interwoven into geography, politics, and social norms of ancient Greece. Each city-state often had a patron deity who provided protection and guidance - Athena being Athens while Apollo watched over Delphi - each god or goddess played an essential part in shaping cultural identity through civic and cultural identity of cities throughout Greece.

The pantheon wasn't simply an eclectic assortment of divine personalities; it also boasted an intricate hierarchy and relationship network. Zeus, as King of the Gods, reigned supreme, yet there were challenges to his rule from other deities in his realm. He faced rebellions from other gods, family drama and maintaining cosmic order - it's like watching an epic soap opera where not just broken hearts are on the line but often our very survival as a planet is also at stake! Demeter and Artemis were powerful goddesses who exercised significant influence, yet operated in areas considered less political. Demeter was revered as the goddess of agriculture with her own temples and major festival called Eleusinian Mysteries that played an essential role in Greek religious life.

Why does all this intricacy and complexity matter? Understanding the intricate dynamics of the Greek pantheon provides invaluable insight into their society-- where divine and mortal realms were inextricably linked, myths were used as reflections of daily life, human flaws, societal norms and gods were seen not just as distant figures but as entities which directly intervened into human affairs such as Athena aiding Odysseus through his perilous journey home or Apollo bestowing prophecy upon Delphi.

When discussing Greek gods and goddesses, it can be tempting to generalize about them according to their domains--for instance, Poseidon rules over seafaring while Ares reigns supreme in warfare--but that would do a disservice to their unique personas and multifaceted identities. Hermes was more than just the messenger god; he also represented trade, boundaries and guides into the Underworld. While Hephaestus may often get overshadowed by more glamorous deities, he certainly deserves equal consideration as an amazing god in his own right. As the god of blacksmiths, craftsmen, and fire, Herakleito is seen as an icon of creativity and ingenuity; traits highly esteemed in Greek culture. His limp was considered a deformity at one point in antiquity; this added complexity to his character that defied Greece's ideal of physical perfection.

This idea that gods had multiple characteristics leads to another crucial insight: these gods did not remain static beings throughout history; rather, they changed over time with society's values and needs. Aphrodite was originally worshiped as goddess of love and fertility but she took on more martial elements after moving to Sparta with its militaristic culture; similarly, Hades evolved over time from being only associated with death into becoming more fearsome over time - much like an ongoing TV series where characters could develop over time! It's almost like watching an ongoing series with characters changing over years or centuries!

An aspect of Greek religious thought that makes its pantheon particularly intriguing is how it connects with other mythologies. Greek gods did not exist in isolation - through conquest, trade and cultural exchange they mingled with gods from other lands such as Isis from Egypt who was worshiped as an Egyptian goddess associated with magic and healing in Greece while Zeus Ammon represented his syncretic union with Amun from Egypt - further enriching their pantheon and demonstrating their adaptable nature.

Several Greek deities had counterparts in Roman mythology; Zeus as Jupiter, Ares as Mars etc. Though these duality figures may appear identical at first glance, their Roman counterparts often adopted different traits and characteristics due to Rome's unique cultural milieu - evidence that shows just how adaptable and far-reaching mythological figures could be, transcending geographical and cultural boundaries and becoming universal archetypes.

Lastly, the Greek pantheon provides an accurate reflection of human psychology. Each god or goddess represents different aspects of our psyche - Athena personifies wisdom and strategy, Dionysus stands for unrestrained emotion, while Hermes stands for quick wit and adaptability. Carl Jung and other psychoanalysts have explored how these mythical figures embody universal human traits and concerns, attesting to their ongoing relevance.

1.1.1 The Major Gods and Goddesses and Their Relationships

If Mount Olympus had a Facebook, its relationship status would perpetually be "It's complicated." Zeus and Hera represent an ideal power couple at the top of this divine food chain; however, don't let their titles of "King" and "Queen of the Gods" deceive you into thinking they represent marital bliss. Hera, often depicted as an overbearing wife, represents matrimony and childbirth as complex concepts. Her fury often arises not solely out of jealousy but out of an intention to protect the values she represents: marriage and family life. Zeus was known for his infidelity but also played an essential role in maintaining justice and law among gods and mortals alike. Their relationship was crucial in setting the stage for relationships among Olympians as a whole.

Athena and Apollo form another intellectual couple that share an inextricable bond through wisdom and arts.

Though Athena was not given a mother in life, her intelligence often lends towards masculine pursuits such as war; while Apollo, as god of prophecy and music, has both masculine and feminine energies represented through his twin sister Artemis who rules over moonlit wilderness areas while Apollo reigns supreme in civilization; their bond captures perfectly balance by harmonizing chaotic and orderly aspects of life into one harmonious whole.

Demeter and Persephone's relationship serves as the ultimate example of balanced parent-child relations, depicting nature's cycles through her seasonal visits to the Underworld for Persephone to return. Demeter's grief during Persephone's absence creates winter on Earth while her joy upon her daughter's return ushers in spring, symbolizing familial love as part of nature.

Another intriguing relationship to consider is between Poseidon, god of the sea, and Zeus, his more prominent brother. Both wielded immense power; however, Poseidon's realm was limited to ocean waters and considered secondary in comparison to that of heaven and earth. This led to some type of sibling rivalry, with Poseidon continually trying to assert his importance more - even conspiring with other gods against Zeus (though that coup was unsuccessful). Their tension reflected ancient Greek perceptions of nature: sea was both sustenance for land creatures while providing unpredictable forces; subordinate yet integral components.

And don't overlook the fascinating relationships among major gods and "lesser" gods and goddesses; for example, Hermes serves as messenger to each Olympian god and interacts closely with them all, from Zeus who wants him to execute orders; Apollo sees him more as mischievous younger brother; Hermes even takes souls of the dead to Hades who rules over Hades in Hades' Underworld realm-revealing a complex relationship encompassing life and death.

One of the most fascinating aspects of divine relationships is their expression through legends and myths. You may know of the Trojan War, but do you know its cause was divine discord during a wedding that degenerated into a beauty contest among Hera, Athena and Aphrodite? Talk about family drama with world-changing consequences! These alliances and rivalries among gods don't simply provide for great stories but have actually altered destiny and guided civilizations from ancient Greece to Rome and beyond.

Not all stories of gods wreaking havoc involve them creating mayhem; often their collaboration saves the day. Typhon threatened to destroy the world until, through collective action from all gods despite rivalries and disagreements among themselves, they managed to subdue him. This illustrates that while individual deities had their spheres of influence and roles to fulfill, they all played part in a larger cosmic order; when combined together these skills become most potent.

The gods also formed relationships outside Olympus with mortals and heroes beyond Olympus itself, including mortals and heroes like Hercules and Perseus. Although these interactions sometimes led to complicated scenarios (Zeus is still being teased about all his dalliances!), they also gave rise to heroes like Hercules and Perseus as demigods who stood as living bridges between human and divine realms; these demigods endured hardships, completed quests, accomplished great deeds while being susceptible to human frailties - stories both cautionary tales as sources of inspiration demonstrating what humanity could accomplish given a little divine help!

Never let it be forgotten that gods had significant interactions not just with their own kind but also with beings thought to be monstrous, like Titans, Gorgons and Cyclopes. Athena's rivalry with Poseidon for patronage of Athens led to its creation, the olive tree; but also to Medusa being born as well as Cyclopes -- monstrous-looking creatures known for being master artisans. Such relationships demonstrate that Greek gods did not exist in a simplistic world of good and evil; their world was more complex, often blurred by moral ambiguity. Such relationships add an additional layer of complexity to existing relationships and remind us that family can come in unexpected forms.

Another amazing aspect is the psychological depth that these relationships add to gods. Rather than being simply one-dimensional figures of power, gods come alive through emotional interactions; from love, jealousy, pride to insecurity and vengefulness - making them relatable mirrors for human emotions and relationships - especially among a culture which prioritized virtues like wisdom, bravery and temperance - making these gods rich sources of ethical discussion topics as well as psychological terrain to explore and debate upon.

1.1.2 Lesser-Known Deities: The Complete Family Tree

Now that we have acquainted ourselves with Olympus' most iconic figures, let's turn our focus toward its lesser-known deities; those often unnoticed but vital members of ancient Greek religion who played vital roles in shaping myths and belief systems of antiquity - but are rarely featured on magazine covers such as Olympian Vogue! Perhaps here you may discover an unexpected favorite character to root for among this array!

Hestia, the goddess of hearth and home, often stands in the shadows of her more flashy siblings. Although Hestia may not make headlines with spectacular battles or romantic liaisons, her domain was vitally important for the well-being of households - her hearth served as the center of family life and her flame was forbidden to go out in temples, symbolizing not just physical warmth but emotional comfort as well. Many households dedicated their first offerings for Hestia each day as proof of her significance to daily Greek life.

Eileithyia was revered as the goddess of childbirth in ancient Greece. Childbirth can be a dangerous undertaking, so having Eileithyia by your side was often seen as essential. Women giving birth would often invoke her during labor and believe in her power to both prolong and shorten the pain associated with childbirth. Temples dedicated to Eileithyia could be found throughout Greece, and ritual offerings often involved olives or cheese as symbols of nourishment and life - so although she might not wield thunderbolts or ride chariots across sky, her role was just as vital in keeping our society functioning effectively!

Hephaestus, the god of fire, blacksmiths and craftsmen is an example of an underdog tale who triumphed despite immense difficulty. After being cast off Mount Olympus by Hera due to his imperfections and being rejected from Mount Olympus altogether for them, Hephaestus rose once more, creating his own palace with mechanical servants of his own; these creations had lasting impacts both divine and mortal realms alike - including Achilles' armor as well as Pandora herself!

Dionysus may be better known today than ever, but did you know he was initially considered a lesser god? The god of wine, pleasure and revelry had to work hard for his spot on Mount Olympus - starting by being born to a mortal mother who was tricked into asking to see Zeus in his true form and was incinerated (ouch!) afterwards; being stitched back into Zeus' thigh until ready to "reborn" once more - making his mortal origins at odds with other gods but his charm made him immensely popular among both Gods and mortals alike!

Let us also not forget Thanatos and Hypnos, the Greek twin gods of death and sleep respectively. Though these gods may sound grim, they played pivotal roles in human existence: Thanatos was not considered evil but simply part of life itself while his brother Hypnos offered relief for mortals worn down from labor or sorrow as well as an avenue for escape. These deities along with Nyx, goddess of the night represent less visible aspects of human experience that cannot be overlooked.

Now take a sip of water as we take a journey into the realm of Nymphs--minor goddesses of nature usually associated with specific places or landforms such as rivers, mountains, or forests. Ever hear of Echo? She was an Npmh cursed to repeat everything she heard due to Hera. Tragically enough, Echo crosses paths with Narcissus' story in an unforgettable tale about love and vanity that holds many lessons for us today.

Regarding gods with specific roles, have you met Aeolus yet? He's known as the Keeper of Winds; his duty was to create or control storms. Odysseus had an interesting dynamic with Aeolus; we'll save that discussion for later chapters! Needless to say, Aeolus didn't command quite the same respect as Olympian gods but try sailing without his blessing and see where you get!

Let's jig along to the Muses! While you might know them from popular culture, did you know there are nine of them altogether, each responsible for different forms of art and science? Clio was known to represent history while Urania represented astronomy; their mother Mnemosyne represented memory - important in keeping oral traditions alive such as myths that we enjoy learning more about now. So next time inspiration strikes you - thank a Muse!

Hecate, the goddess of magic, crossroads, and the moon was an intriguing figure in mythology. Being a triple deity gave Hecate multiple identities depending on her roles - women especially revered her because of her power to grant or withhold women's wishes concerning childbirth and family matters - even Zeus himself respected her abilities! That should speak volumes.

Gods and Goddesses of the Natural World

1.1.3 Gods and Goddesses of the Natural World

Ancient Greeks didn't just venerate gods of epic quests or cosmic justice - they also revered those connected with nature - such as goddesses associated with earth, seas and sky - to recognize divine forces everywhere around them and within themselves. While such divinities might not have inspired as many epic tales about them, their role was essential in daily life for ancients who relied heavily on nature for survival - so let's go on an Olympian nature walk together!

On our journey we begin with Gaia, the original Earth Mother. Before your mind jumps to Zeus and his crew, let me remind you that Gaia was not unlike Zeus in that she gave rise to all creation - be it sky, mountains or sea - she gave life. Gaia wasn't known for directly interfering in human affairs - rather, eruptions such as volcanoes were seen as signals from Gaia about how she felt about certain situations (think earthquakes!). However if upset by Gaia she would certainly let loose--think earthquakes!

Poseidon reigned over the sea. Though well-known, not many know he was also the god of horses - hence why you might see depictions with them! He not only ruled over seas and storms, but was believed to have an effectful presence in daily life, particularly for nations of seafarers such as ancient Greeks who worshiped him with offerings including fish or even sacrifices made specifically to ensure safe passage across water.

As we take to the skies, we come upon Aeolus' lesser-known cousins: Zephyrus, Notus, Boreas and Eurus - each responsible for one particular wind direction. Zephyrus was often depicted as being kind-hearted while Boreas, on the other hand, could often be considered unpleasant company at summer parties! These lesser-known winds interacted with Aeolus in such ways that it affected weather patterns, sailing conditions, commerce agriculture and daily life itself - so much so that many things could change dramatically!

Don't forget Helios and Selene - gods of the sun and moon before Apollo and Artemis entered the picture. Helios rode his chariot across the sky every day, pulling the sun along behind. He served as an observer over earth below while Selene provided more than just night-light; she had her own unique set of powers that affected everything from menstruation cycles to crop growth throughout her phases.

Water, sky and earth may all be obvious concepts; yet what about seasons? Meet the Horae goddesses; lesser-known deities who ruled nature from spring's first blossom to winter's final flake. While they might not receive as much recognition as Demeter or Persephone do now, their role in agriculture was significant: not only did they dictate changing seasons but they also served as watchmen on Olympus to ensure time passed as scheduled.
Let's continue our exploration with Pan, god of the wild, shepherds, and flocks.

Half-man/half-goat in appearance, Pan was the life and soul of any party in the wilderness he hosted; playing his pan flute and dancing while instilling "panic"--from which even its name comes--into enemy combatants during battles. Even though he was considered a lesser god he made an impressionable mark upon various aspects of rural life as well as natural phenomena.

As we sail down rivers and streams, let us not overlook the Naiads and Nereids - water nymphs of freshwater and the sea respectively--who were believed to affect everything from water quality to fish abundance. In ancient Greece they were highly revered, often offering gifts at natural springs or wells to please them; their waters could even be sacred places associated with specific Naiads; disturbing their waters would incur divine punishment.

Ever wondered why bees work so hard? Look no further! Aristaeus was an obscure yet busy minor god responsible for overseeing beekeeping, cheese production and certain forms of animal husbandry. Although less powerful than his counterparts, Aristaeus still played an integral part in these industries' livelihoods; Greek farmers would pray to Aristaeus alongside Demeter as part of daily worship rituals.

Next is Hestia, goddess of the hearth and home. While her realm may seem small compared to forests or oceans, do not underestimate her importance; after all, hearths were at the core of Greek homes for warmth, cooking, family unity and family cohesiveness. Her eternal flame in temples represented community well-being while seeking her blessing was common practice when building new dwellings.

Eileithyia was considered to be an invaluable figure during childbirth in ancient Greece due to the risks involved with childbirth - temples were dedicated to her all over Greece as rituals and sacrifices were performed for safe delivery; she would either loosen a bolt to release child or tighten it fasten a bolt based on whether she felt pleased or insulted during gestation.

1.1.4 How the Greek Gods Reflect Human Nature

Today we delve further into this fascinating mythological tapestry by asking one thought-provoking question: Do the Greek gods reflect human nature in any tangible way? Imagine this--why would gods act jealous, kind, vengeful or loving when they should be divine beings? Well, the answer to that one lies deep within these stories themselves - ancient Greeks saw gods not as remote entities but as amplified reflections of human traits and tendencies reflected back onto themselves - prepare yourself as this journey takes us on an unprecedented voyage of exploration!

Take, for instance, Zeus as an example: this all-powerful ruler of gods had an array of illicit affairs and an unpredictable temperament which left his followers shaking in their boots - far from being an epitome of moral virtue! Yet his relatability lies precisely here - his flaws made him all the more relatable! Zeus represented both aspirations and risks associated with power and leadership for ancient Greeks who knew all too well how holding onto power could bring both benefits and drawbacks; therefore painting Zeus with both capabilities and liabilities so he became not so much an exaggerated expression of what humans could become given authority; rather he served as an allegorical expression of what human could become given such power and control!

Hera, Zeus's Queen and Goddess of Marriage. Her unwavering loyalty to Zeus speaks volumes about society at that time; Hera wasn't simply passive when his affairs occurred - she actively engaged in their escapades by attacking his mistresses and offspring with an extreme level of vindictiveness that betrayed their constraints and expectations for women living under patriarchy - her actions being an indication of women navigating social roles and familial duties themselves. Hera serves as a mirror image to human condition especially among female characters such as herself who navigate the complexity of social roles and familial duties within society - something all women experience first-hand today when trying to negotiate roles and familial duties within society itself.

Athena, the goddess of wisdom and war, represents an intriguing paradox with great significance. Athena embodies an equilibrium between intellect and action - reflecting Greek ideals of "arete", or excellence in all things - not simply smarts but tactical brilliance, ethical understanding, practical application. She stands as an embodiment of philosophy-warrior wisdom: knowledge without courage is meaningless.

Ares is the God of War! In contrast to Athena, who represents wisdom and strength in wartime, Ares represents violence with reckless abandon. Yet his presence atop Olympus was deliberate: Ares embodies raw emotions associated with conflict ranging from bloodlust and terror. Ares represents human nature's primal instinct for aggression and dominance; even today these instincts continue to shape history, kingdoms are won and lost, as well as global politics today - Ares serves as a stark reminder that these instincts still reside within us all!

At last, let's briefly visit Dionysus, god of wine, theater and ecstasy. At first glance, Dionysus appears to be all about having fun; yet dig deeper and you discover an intricate god who explores boundaries between pleasure and pain, sanity and madness through wild revels and passionate outbursts; his myths serve both as cautionary tales as well as celebratory tales to remind us about life's dualities between restraint and indulgence as well as reason and emotion within us all.

Apollo, the god of music, prophecy and healing offers another intriguing window into our collective psyche. He often represents balance within both body, mind and soul - reflecting our pursuit for inner harmony in body, mind and soul. Apollo serves as a reminder that excess can bring temporary pleasure while balance provides long-term fulfillment. Apollo's dual nature--sometimes inspiring but other times punishing--mirrors our own struggle for moral and aesthetic balance in life.

Now let's enter the world of love and desire with Aphrodite. She symbolizes both beauty and attraction while embodying all the chaos and unpredictability associated with love, be it romantic, familial or platonic; her myths cover it all! Aphrodite doesn't simply serve as an object of affection - rather she serves as a guidebook to show both wonder and folly that can result from succumbing to our desires.

Hermes, the messenger god and master of thieves who guides souls to the afterlife. This dynamic character personifies human identity through change. With his many roles, Hermes serves as an appropriate symbol for today's rapidly changing society that prizes adaptability and resourcefulness. As with Hermes himself, we often wear many hats ourselves--sometimes literally! In him we see our own hustle; between responsibilities and aspirations there are trade-offs made along the way which mirror what happens in real life.

Let's add a dash of the macabre by discussing Hades, god of the underworld. Although often depicted as a villainous figure in modern adaptations, he governed one of humanity's inevitable aspects - death. More than just mortality though, Hades symbolizes our feelings about loss, the afterlife, and what awaits us beyond this life. Love him or fear him - Hades personifies our existential questions regarding what lies beyond this life.

Let us also consider Demeter, goddess of agriculture and fertility. Demeter serves as an iconic embodiment of nature as an allegory for human experience, through her mythological deity Persephone's abduction: joy vs sorrow; birth vs decay; life vs death. She serves as an allegory for our ability to overcome life's seasons and emerge renewed from them all.

1.2. Heroes, Antiheroes, and Monsters: Mortal Encounters

1.2.1 The Exploits of Hercules, Odysseus, and More

Where should we even begin when discussing Greek heroes? They are undisputed icons of ancient mythology; their adventures filled with action, drama and life lessons can't help but draw you in. So let's begin our exploration with Hercules (or Heracles in Spanish if that's more your style).

Hercules was the son of Alcmena and Zeus - two individuals whom, as Zeus is their God father figure, could probably claim parenthood! But right away Hercules faced immense pressure due to Hera (Zeus' actual wife) harboring strong animosity for him. From strangling serpents in his crib to undertaking the 12 Labors, Hercules embarked on an extraordinary lifelong quest for redemption and glory. These labors weren't your average chores - these were Herculean challenges meant to test his resolve! Cleaning the Augean Stables in one day, capturing and subduing the Golden Hind, and subduing the Nemean Lion--each endeavor was more than an act of strength; each was an exploration into oneself and understanding of human morality.

Consider Hercules' labors of capturing the Erymanthian Boar; this wasn't simply about catching an unwieldy beast; there were layers of themes to consider such as environmental harmony and pride and arrogance - just two examples that come to mind here! Hercules symbolizes man's ongoing fight against external challenges as well as internal struggles; this reminds us that heroism must remain part of our everyday lives to achieve true heroism.

Let's move onto Odysseus (Ulysses), one of the early champions of "work smarter, not harder". Remember the Trojan Horse? He created it! Odysseus had the mental agility needed to navigate complex challenges more effectively than Hercules could, bench pressing mountains with ease. Odysseus' story unfolds in the Odyssey; after conquering Troy he embarks on an arduous 10-year journey back home to Ithaca and to regain the throne from suitors that have attempted to usurp it from him. As he progresses on his quest, he encounters fantastical beings such as Cyclops; navigates treacherous waters filled with man-eating monsters such as Scylla and Charybdis; and battles against alluring beings such as Circe and Sirens. Odysseus' story isn't only geographical; it is psychological and emotional as well. Each trial tests different aspects of his character--his intellect, loyalty, resilience--holding up a mirror to our own vulnerabilities and strengths. His journey shows us how life's journey, like Odysseus', presents us with tests which test our wit, integrity and spirit.

Before we breeze past this segment, let's highlight one more hero: Achilles. His name has become a byword for unrivaled strength--with one exception being an Achilles' heel of course! Best known for his role in the Trojan War where he seemed virtually invincible against warriors from both sides, Achilles is most revered today. Achilles was not without his emotional rollercoasters. Take Patroclus, his best friend and confidant whose death sent Achilles spiraling into an intense fury that nearly resulted in catastrophe. He rose quickly to power, slaughtering Trojans mercilessly. Yet Achilles' true legacy lies in his humanity: for all his apparent invincibility, he was still profoundly human, subject to anger, sorrow and mortality just like us all. His tale compels us to consider our dual natures--public hero versus private individual-- invincible yet vulnerable.

Now on our agenda: Jason (no relation to horror movies!). Jason embarked on a quest for the Golden Fleece, and his story stands in stark contrast to those of Hercules or Odysseus in terms of sheer muscle showoff or strategic brilliance; instead it introduces another kind of hero --a collaborative hero--while also providing some unique character insight. Yup, Jason recognized the value of teamwork. To win his prized fleece, he assembled his Argonauts: an eclectic group composed of warriors, adventurers and even some demi-gods (!) Incorporating nautical adventures, dragon-fighting (because why not!) and dramatic rescues, Jason is most noteworthy for assembling diverse talents under his leadership rather than acting solo as show stopper; his story shows us that some quests require multiple people working together as one.

Let's shift our focus onto Oedipus. Oedipus has long been seen as an antihero due to his unfortunate circumstances; an event which would break even the strongest among us down. Oedipus accidentally killed his father and married his mother; an event which made even the strongest among us fall apart! Oedipus' tale unfolds like a tragic opera, touching upon themes such as destiny, free will, human limitation and understanding limitations. However, unlike most heroes Oedipus doesn't fight monsters or embark upon grand quests; rather, his battle takes place within himself as he confronts his unfathomable fate! His story makes you think!

Ever heard of Perseus? He's yet another offspring of Zeus (wonder why?!?) and an ordinary mortal woman, known for slaying Medusa the Gorgon - his claim to fame being to overcome her serpent-hairs with technology; specifically his shield's double function as a mirror that helped avoid looking directly into Medusa's eyes, which would otherwise turn everyone into stone! Perseus' story provides us with lessons on courage and cunning - showing how heroes don't always rely on brute strength - sometimes you must outwit obstacles like Medusa yourself!

No need to panic: we're not leaving this epic saga without touching on some truly incredible women who also dominated the hero scene in their own ways, such as Atalanta who could outrun anyone and was also part of the Argonauts crew. Her story adds much-needed gender diversity by showing that heroism doesn't belong exclusively to men.

Antigone is another example of courage who showed hers by standing up against an unfair law to ensure her brother received a proper burial, showing us that being heroic doesn't always involve physical combat; sometimes it means resisting unjust systems and fighting for what you believe to be right despite going against family or nation.

At last! Our epic journey through heroes, antiheroes, and monsters should have left you both informed and eager to explore further. Whether through Hercules' brute strength, Odysseus' tactical nous, or Antigone's moral courage - Greek mythos offers something for everyone!

1.2.2 Tragic Heroes: The Tales of Orpheus and Icarus

Now it's time for our second tragic hero tales--Orpheus and Icarus--to unfold before us. Prepare yourself, these stories are sure to tug at your heartstrings! These Greek mythological characters stand out due to their tragically human flaws and misplaced ambition, teaching us that even heroes are vulnerable.

Let's begin by talking about Orpheus, the rock star of ancient Greece. No kidding; Orpheus was an amazing musician whose melodic talent could enchant animals and even move inanimate objects such as trees or rivers backwards - an incredible feat that required divine-level artistry and not mere talent.

Orpheus' life took an unfortunate turn when he fell in love with Eurydice. She became his muse, his everything - when she died suddenly he was heartbroken - so much so that he decided to do the unthinkable: descend into Hades' Underworld to bring back Eurydice! Most people are terrified by its darkness but not Orpheus - he braved its depths with nothing more than his lyre in hand and an undying love. Many others shy away from its depths while Orpheus came straight in armed only with his music in hopes that even Hades himself might succumb to its spell and bring Eurydice back home again!

Things started off well; his music melted the hearts of Hades and Persephone, who granted his request with one condition: Orpheus could lead Eurydice back out into the living world, but could not look back until they had both exited the Underworld together. Tension was high until anxiety overtook him moments before reaching the surface; Orpheus turned back, leaving Eurydice lost forever behind him. His story serves as a cautionary tale against doubting ourselves too quickly when love grows deeper within us all too fast.

Now we come to Icarus - that classic tale of youthful ambition gone horribly awry. Born to Daedalus, an extraordinary craftsman responsible for designing King Minos of Crete's Labyrinth. To evade Minos' anger, Daedalus created two sets of wings made from feathers and wax for himself and Icarus to fly away from Crete and find freedom, although Daedalus warn Icarus not to fly too close to the sun or else his wax wings would melt.

Though flying seems simple enough, Icarus was soon overwhelmed by his newfound freedom and rode the thrill higher and higher despite warnings from his father. We know how that ended: the sun melted his wax and Icarus plummeted into the sea; turning what could have been an inspiring escape story into an insightful lesson on human limitations and hubris.

After his tragic loss of Eurydice, Orpheus was distraught. His grief was so great that he abandoned women altogether and wandered alone while playing sorrowful tunes on his lyre - an example of how sudden, profound losses can alter who we are radically. Orpheus' actions speak volumes about this idea - their story encourages us to contemplate just how deeply love, loss and regret can alter lives.

Now back to Icarus: his fall wasn't simply into the ocean - it became iconic, symbolizing reckless ambition, youthful foolishness and the consequences of not listening to wise advice. His tale is often used as a moral lesson about moderation and being mindful when trying to surpass human limits - however isn't this story also an important reminder of how youthful exuberance and dreams may sometimes be crushed under reality?

Orpheus and Icarus provide us with important cautionary tales. Orpheus' tale underscores how fragile human emotions can be and the lasting repercussions of an irrevocable decision made quickly and impulsively, while Icarus stands as a timeless warning against disregarding wisdom from previous generations. Yet isn't it fascinating that their stories continue to resonate today? These tragic heroes have become immortalized for all their flaws and failures, reminding us all that imperfection is part of human experience.

Just when we thought the chapter on Orpheus and Icarus had ended, let's pause for a moment to consider their impact in contemporary culture. You would be amazed to know that their tragic deaths haven't just faded into history but have permeated literature, music and scientific discourse alike.

Consider, for instance, the term "Orphic," which has come to symbolize anything melodious or charming since Orpheus first showed his musical gifts. This linguistic evolution prompts us to ask: how have myths influenced our language? Our daily expression often bears witness to stories dating back centuries or millennia.

Switching gears again, Icarus lives on in a different way: as the "Icarus Complex," an area of psychology which refers to individuals with an obsession for catastrophic failure or grandiose failure. This phenomenon shows just how far myths can reach beyond bedtime stories; they have come into psychology as archetypes for understanding human behavior.

These myths have been adapted and reinterpreted into various forms, from operas and ballets to comic books and video games, yet that does not negate their status as classics: each version sheds new light on previously unsuspected areas of myth.

Myths tell tales about individual characters and their fates, yet also speak directly to us as individuals - their collective hopes, fears, dreams and nightmares all reflecting a real-life world in which we exist every day.

1.2.3 Iconic Monsters: Medusa, Minotaur, and Chimera

Let us introduce the monsters of Greek mythology--those iconic, timeless characters who continue to haunt our dreams and excite our imaginations centuries after they first appeared. But these "monsters" don't exist just for nightmares or mythological embellishment - they contain deep cultural significance and psychological insight! Let's dive deeper and uncover some of their tales: Medusa, Minotaur and Chimera will be on our radar today.

Let's begin with Medusa: forget what you know of her in popular culture; chances are, there may be misperceptions about this snake-haired Gorgon. No longer an ordinary monster to be killed off, Medusa stands as a warning against the dangers and powers of femininity - or perhaps she represents its victimhood altogether? Her tale offers chilling insight into gaze, objectification and how society perceives women.

Did you know that Medusa was once an attractive maiden? Her beauty became her undoing after desecrating Athena's temple; not just a punishment for herself but a warning against hubris and disrespect toward the gods.

Medusa inspired fear and respect in equal measures; her power lay in both petrifying, protecting and defying those around her. When Perseus used Medusa's severed head to rescue Andromeda from being captured by Kronos, and set it on Athena's protective Aegis shield as an emblem. Even amongst her monstrosity lay some sort of reverence.

Let's switch gears. Let's talk about the Minotaur, that half-bull, half-human creature imprisoned within the Labyrinth who serves as an antagonist for Theseus to defeat; in reality he represents many fears and anxieties for us today--of hybridity, imprisonment and violent tendencies in society as a whole.

The Minotaur is born of Queen Pasiphae's unholy union with a bull, as divine punishment for King Minos' prideful arrogance before the gods. What this suggests is that its creation stands as an embodiment of arrogance before them as well as of forbidden desires gone wrong.

As is evident from their stories, Medusa and Minotaur stories offer more questions than answers. They force us to ponder our moral compasses as well as confront darker corners of human nature and social taboos. Even today these myths continue to play an integral part in collective storytelling, art creation, and even our fears.

Oh man! If Medusa and Minotaur were fascinating creatures, wait till we discover this strange, bizarre beast: Chimera! Imagine having an animal body with goat ears sprouting out the back, goat head sprouting from its back, and an serpent for its tail: this might look like something out of a fever dream but trust me: the Chimera is more than an obscure fantasy creature; it represents all of life's unpredictable forces that arise within it.

The Chimera hails from Lycia in what is now Turkey and should never be understood in its original sense; rather it represents natural disasters such as volcanic eruptions. Additionally, its fire-breathing aspect serves as an allegory for volatile geothermal activities in Lycia.

As may come as a shock to some, Chimera also represents duality and contradiction. A lion represents strength while goats often represent fertility, while serpents are associated with wisdom or cunning - when combined all together this metaphor for reality becomes even more intricate and meaningful.

At least, that was what Bellerophon thought! With his horse Pegasus at his side and guided by Athena's wisdom, Bellerophon used its wings to slay the Chimera from above - teaching an important lesson about conquering chaos through courage and divine guidance.

So there you have it--the captivating tapestry that is Greek mythical monsters. Each monster contains layers of meanings, prompting questions about morality, humanity, and where the boundary lines between the two exist. If someone casually mentions "chimeras" or if you come across snake-haired villains in video games that feature such monsters, keep in mind there is much depth hidden underneath those scales and fangs.

Before we conclude this mythical menagerie, let's pause for a moment and think about why these stories have endured for millennia - from ancient myths and movies all the way to contemporary ones. Is it because these monsters appeal to our love of all things fantastical? Perhaps, but more likely because these stories serve as mirrors; reflecting our deepest fears, ambitions and even social norms. Take for instance the Minotaur as a tragic result of human hubris and divine displeasure - isn't this an unforgettable reminder of what happens as a consequence?

Medusa, once an exquisite priestess who became a Gorgon due to divine punishment, can serve as a poignant symbol of power dynamics between genders. While she can often be dismissed as just another monster to be defeated, Medusa represents both complexity and peril associated with gender relations in society.

But these tales don't just explain or entertain; they serve as warnings, ethical fables, and political critiques that offer something deeper: when you read beneath their scales and fangs or labyrinthine mazes to explore what it means to be human, not simply reading myths but engaging in an age-old dialogue about being a part of humanity.

1.2.4 The Human Element: Morals and Lessons

By now you have met the gods with their antics, explored mythical landscapes with heroic figures who may or may not live up to expectations, and encountered creatures from your wildest nightmares (or fantasies). But let's pause a bit and dive deep into one of the most fascinating layers of Greek mythology: morals and lessons delivered via these myths that deepen human understanding - and let me warn you, things get very compelling at this point!

These myths don't exist just to amuse, however; rather, Greek myths were intended as vehicles for exploring all sides of humanity - good and bad alike. One classic example is Prometheus who stole fire from the gods to give to humanity; on its surface this story may depict rebellion; however if you look deeper you'll discover themes such as self-sacrifice, knowledge thirstiness and resistance against authoritarian rule.

Let's turn our focus toward Pandora. Many know her by her box--or rather, its original depiction: the jar--which holds all sorts of delights inside it. Don't misunderstand: Pandora represents more than an innocent curiosity gone awry: her story delves deep into human emotion and curiosity, when she opened that container and unleashed suffering into the world yet also offered hope to people everywhere despite hardship and tragedy.

Remember the story of King Midas? He foolishly desired that everything he touched would turn to gold, only to discover that not even his most treasured daughter could escape this terrible curse! What an eye-opening example of greed and the dangers associated with not considering our desires!

Not all myths require major figures and names as examples to draw lessons. Sometimes it's the lesser-known stories, like Narcissus' story of being entranced by his own reflection and becoming obsessed, that can speak volumes. Consider his tragic demise - an allegory for the dangers associated with extreme self-absorption and extreme love of oneself.

Never forget Arachne, the skilled weaver who dared to challenge Athena but was ultimately turned into a spider for her hubris. A powerful tale about pride can lead to one's downfall as well as exploring skill, artistry and the dynamics between mortals and gods - A compelling and thought-provoking tale!

Stories have long offered us insight into the fine line between right and wrong, wisdom and folly, yet there's still so much more we can unpack from these tales. Think back to Achilles? Almost invincible at first, yet vulnerable at his heel (and, quite frankly, ego). These characters remind us of human life's inherent fragility - of all our imperfections as individuals that make us all so human in terms of experience.

Imagine an epic tale like The Trojan War; its narrative brings together themes of love, betrayal, honor and the devastating effects of pride and stubbornness in one captivating saga. Like an ideal multi-season drama series without Netflix subscription! Furthermore, it introduces the concept of "Pyrrhic Victory", in which victory was gained at too great a price to truly count as victory.

Myths don't just focus on doom-and-gloom; they also celebrate cleverness, ingenuity and perseverance. Take Odysseus as an example - his story illustrates that clever thinking can sometimes trump brawn; his life lessons teach us that brains outwit brawn when faced with difficult situations.

Theseus, who negotiated the Labyrinth with only a simple ball of thread, is an example of resourcefulness and problem-solving that shows you don't always require supernatural abilities to become a hero. Myths like Theseus serve as life guides by offering wisdom on how we might navigate difficult career paths or relationships more successfully.

But what of the often-overlooked yet equally important female characters found in Greek myths? Figures like Penelope represent both faithfulness and cunning - waiting for Odysseus for twenty years while defusing suits through her cleverness - or Atalanta who could outwit most male heroes? These female figures don't simply serve as side stories; their presence adds depth and dimension to Greek mythology's rich tapestry of values and character traits celebrated.

Have we exhausted ethical navel-gazing yet? Not by any stretch of the imagination! There's plenty more nuance and detail to uncover beyond what we've discussed here; hopefully this has provided you with a deeper appreciation of how these "simple" myths can have so much weight behind them; not simply as pictures from long ago but as mirrors to ourselves that force us to consider human nature as it unfolds over time.

Have you ever considered the myth of Prometheus, the Titan who stole fire from the gods and gave it to humanity? At first glance, you may think he is doing humanity a favor by sharing his knowledge. Yet look deeper, and you'll see that this story explores themes such as defiance, innovation and power dynamics - while providing us with insight into human ethics.

Consider this: Prometheus' act gave humans the tools they needed to survive and thrive, yet also gave us weapons with which we can destroy themselves. Fire can cook your meals while providing warmth; yet, its powerful flames have the capacity to consume forests and cities alike - providing us with both benefits as well as ethical considerations that must be considered when moving forward technologically or intellectually. It serves as a potent metaphor for technological and intellectual progress while simultaneously raising moral dilemmas that come along with it.

Who could forget the tale of Pandora's Box, in which curiosity led her to open a box (it was really more like a jar) which unleashed evil upon the world while simultaneously sealing hope at its base? In this seemingly straightforward story lie layers upon layers of meaning about curiosity, consequences and hope itself.

So let's not get started on the myth of Narcissus either - that guy who became so mesmerized by his reflection that he died staring at it? This cautionary tale serves as a timely warning about self-obsession and vanity - themes which couldn't be more applicable in our social media-driven culture where likes and followers can seem like validation of oneself.

Myths don't simply exist within one culture or historical era - they have been and continue to be used and adapted in art, literature and philosophy - from Aristotle's teachings through modern day retellings; each generation finds something new to discover while taking lessons away for themselves.

1.3. From Chaos to Cosmos: Creation Myths and Wisdom Tales

1.3.1 The Story of Creation: Emerging from Chaos

Creation stories from the starting point of every mythology; each culture from Greece to Japan offers their unique version of how life, Earth and cosmos came into being. Let's begin with the Greeks. In their imagination, life on Earth began in a state known as "Chaos", where all elements were scattered without form or purpose. Think of this like your messy teenager's room on an epic scale! Chaos doesn't refer to total disorder or confusion as we typically understand it; rather, think of it as Greeks' way of referring to an immaculate, primordial state; it doesn't signify lack of order but more about lacking differentiation between things.

Before we delve into how Earth (Gaia) rose from Chaos or Night (Nyx) and Erebus came into being, it's essential that we acknowledge how similar concepts of Chaos appear elsewhere in mythologies around the world. The Norse cosmos had its "Ginnungagap," while Egyptian mythology started off with an infinite expanse of dark waters known as Nun. Their existence is no mere coincidence; their parallel illustrates their universal nature as human attempts to explain ineffable mysteries by creating stories around them.

Why do many myths begin with nothingness?" Well, here's the key point: this is more than poetic license! Throughout history, thinkers have explored how something could emerge from an inert state or nothingness and then be manifested into tangible form through creation. Even modern cosmology makes note of the age-old concept that something may emerge from nothingness - in other words something can indeed come out of nothingness.' In modern cosmology's theory of inflationary universe expansion called Big Bang theory gives credit to this age-old concept or at least an inert state so different from our current universe that we cannot describe it properly as anything other than nothingness!

Are you familiar with the term 'axis mundi?' It is an archaic term which refers to the connection between Heaven and Earth, usually symbolized in myth by trees, mountains or other natural structures acting as cosmic bridges such as Mount Olympus for Greeks, Yggdrasil in Norse culture and Mount Meru in Hindu culture - these all serve as centers for cosmic significance within their respective cultures but we won't go too deep into that topic here - for now let's just talk about mythology!

Right, let us focus on Chaos and its universal allure. After all, 'Chaos' serves as the blank slate upon which all creation myths can be painted; gods and goddesses who come later to shape humanity from its foundation onward are like artists with unique styles; we call these creators with a capital "C" here because these deities play such an essential role. However, these creators do not simply sit high above us with judgmental eyes looking down from above--indeed they embody both flaws, conflicts and emotions that make up human existence--another topic we will delve into.

As to who created what, we find ourselves faced with an existential conundrum akin to the chicken-and-egg question in myths: who came first: the gods or their world they inhabit? Yet that is precisely the beauty of myths: they don't confine their tales with linear thinking but can sometimes bend time itself around into an intricate dance between creators and creations, where sometimes one becomes another; this can even occur symbolically through ouroboros: a snake which consumes its tail! Symbolising time itself!

Before closing this chapter both literally and metaphorically, let us consider why we, as humans, find so many creation myths so captivating. Perhaps it is to satisfy our curiosity or perhaps it provides insight into the collective psyche of our ancestors by showing how they used emotional and intellectual tools to cope with life's greatest questions. Either way, creation myths remain powerful markers of human creativity as we search for our place within this grand scheme of things.

1.3.2 Pandora's Box and the Concept of Hope

Imagine this: you have the first woman ever created, crafted by gods as part of an elaborate grander plan. But they didn't just randomly put her together: each god gave her specific gifts that helped create her into an amalgam of divine traits and human flaws. Finally, at some point during this storyline she received an unopened jar containing one or more gifts--though no doubt many translations use "box".

"Well, that is just setting her up for failure isn't it?" Perhaps, but that is exactly the point. Pandora's Jar represents our constant struggle between curiosity and obedience, risk and reward, temptation and restraint; all in an ever-evolving game between human will and divine machinations that creates palpable tension - it's like giving someone an immense treasure chest while warning them not to open it! Temptation becomes almost irresistible.

So let's say you don't know the story: Pandora was driven by an irresistible curiosity to open her jar and reveal all the evils of humanity - death, sickness and toil--that have plagued humanity throughout time. However, there was one surprise hidden at the bottom: Elpis, commonly translated as Hope, was present inside! So why would such positive energy reside alongside so much negativity?

Interpretations vary, my friend. Some claim it offers humanity comfort from Pandora's evils; others see it as cruelest joke ever; giving hope when in reality suffering is ever present; yet others believe Hope itself to be one of humanity's greatest adversaries, keeping humans constantly longing yet never fully contented - see why I say this tale is more intricate than it initially appears?

Hope in Pandora provides us with an unprecedented look into how ancient Greeks viewed human nature and life's trials, not simply questioning our virtues and vices but focusing on all that makes us human - whether seen as blessing or curse, Hope captures all aspects of human spirit in its contradictory splendor.

Pandora remains an enduring mythological figure from ancient Greece to Renaissance Europe and today's pop culture, representing human fragility, divine caprice, and our tireless capacity for hope.

Why has this story captured people for so long? Well, for starters it is relatable. Who among us hasn't been tempted by something we should avoid and experienced the negative repercussions? Whether it be as simple as eating an extra piece of cake or binge-watching when they should have been working - our own actions often turn against us and are our greatest obstacles. That is an age-old human condition: We are both our biggest allies and worst adversaries.

However, we should look beyond this story's surface meaning: this tale illustrates the complex relationship between humans and gods - or more generally speaking, any universal force such as fate or karma - as well as questions of free will versus determinism; was Pandora predetermined to open that jar or did she truly have free choice in doing so? What can her decision tell us about ourselves as decision-makers?

Pandora also serves to highlight issues surrounding gender. After all, she was the first woman created as part of a divine plan to bring evil and suffering into the world; feminist interpretations of her story raise valid questions: is this narrative used as an ancient means of placing blame for world problems on women, or could it instead serve as an inspiring story about a powerful female asserting their will despite potential adverse repercussions?

So here we are, exploring this captivating tale in depth. While one could write an entire book just on Pandora's story alone, let's simply appreciate its complexity, duality and continued relevance - not as much a warning story but one full of endless interpretation and dare I say "Hope".

1.3.3 The Role of Fate: The Moirai and their Influence

Greek mythology presents Fate not as some abstract concept but as three very real and rather harsh goddesses known as Moirai: Clotho, Lachesis and Atropos - commonly referred to as Spinner, Allotter and Inflexible respectively. They should be thanked or blamed for all that comes to pass in life--something you should thank--or blame them--accordingly in the Greek mythological universe!

Clotho is the one who creates our lives' threads, envisioning her spinning away on her distaff to craft your reality with unique threads woven by cosmic insight. Each life thread may have different qualities--yours may be strong and resilient while someone else's could be delicate and fray easily--Clotho acts like the ultimate artisan choosing their color, texture and quality with precision.

Lachesis stands next. She acts as the measurer, determining how long each thread--your life--will span. Thus she plays an instrumental role in either prolonging or shortening it. If Clotho serves as artist, Lachesis serves as editor. Taking what is spun from Clotho, Lachesis decides its fit into a grand narrative, how much influence it will exert over it and its place within it.

Do not overlook Atropos: she's the most terrifying of the Moirai because she cuts the thread. There's no bargaining with Atropos when your time on earth has ended: out come her abhorred shears and cut; your earthly chapter comes to an end - Atropos truly gives "cutting ties" new meaning!

Are You Feeling Chills Yet? If not, contemplate the profound implications of Moirai. They go far beyond life and death; they touch upon issues of destiny, agency and human existence itself. Since everything seems predetermined if everything else is predetermined as well - something philosophers have been deliberating over since ancient Greece! Neither you or I are likely to come up with any definitive answers here either but isn't it exhilarating just to consider?

Moirai have become part of culture and language; for instance, have you ever heard someone say: "It was meant to be," or similar phrases? These statements pay homage to the Fates as universal symbols which transcend Greek mythology to appear in various other cultural narratives--even today's parlance and thinking!

But there's much more to discover, since the Moirai are not an isolated phenomenon; they form part of Greek cosmological theory as a whole. Like their Roman equivalents - Parcae or Norns in Norse mythology - these sisters symbolize our interdependence and remind us that individual lives form part of an intricate web where even a slight pull on one thread could change or alter everything completely.

What would the gods think about Moirai? Great question! Even they had to submit to the will of Fates; Zeus himself had limitations set by these seemingly subordinate deities - creating an everlasting checks-and-balances system of sorts, though on an interstellar scale.

This paradox, wherein even the most powerful beings must submit to their destiny as set out by Moirai, opens fascinating avenues of thought. It begs the question-- is true power the heft of thunderbolt or shaping of destiny? Aha--food for thought indeed!

Before moving on, let's also take a moment to acknowledge the Moirai sisters' cultural impact. Their sisters have left an indelible mark not only on ancient texts, but on our modern-day understanding of fate and existence as well. Be it literature, drama or even pop culture references--from Shakespearean plays to Marvel comics comic books to opera performances and blockbuster movies--their legacy underscores our ongoing discussion on fate vs free will in society today.

So, are these ageless sisters comforting or unsettling? That depends on your perspective. On one hand, there may be something soothing in thinking that life has already been set into motion by three cosmic sisters with an affinity for yarn and scissors; it helps take the pressure off! However, on the other hand, it could be unnerving to know you are just an insignificant pawn in their cosmic game!

1.3.4 Tales of Wisdom and Folly: Aesop's Fables

Let's move away from the complex world of predetermined cosmic balance and into Aesop's Fables. Unlike Moirai who deal in absolutes and destinies, Aesop offers stories filled with both wisdom and folly that teach valuable life lessons. Aesop was sort of like ancient world's version of viral sensation; his tales traveled far across borders and generations alike and their appeal lies in how grounded in real experiences we all experience as we struggle through daily experiences that resonated across borders and generations alike - just like his Fables were ground in reality and dilemmas we face everyday - Aesop was the ancient world's version of viral sensation

As an illustration of what I'm speaking of here, consider "The Tortoise and the Hare." You've likely come across this classic tale before; its simple tale offers wisdom that resonates throughout life - slow and steady wins the race, as the story emphasizes. And we all have been both tortoises and hares at certain points! At its core, fables like these serve as mirrors that show our human qualities as well as vices in animal form.

But these tales are more than cutest animal tales; they're morality plays in miniature. And you don't need to be a philosopher to 'get it.' Aesop was masterful at weaving complex ethical and philosophical ideas into stories that any audience could understand; take for instance "The Boy Who Cried Wolf", for instance: its themes don't just address lying; rather they explore credibility, trust and the social contract that bonds communities together - teaching us about human interactions where even small mistakes could cause massive ripples downfalls!

Why are we still talking about stories written over 2 millennia ago (orally passed down over millennia ago)? Because they have staying power. Not just because they've been translated and adapted into various forms of media; their timeless messages about human condition remain as relevant now as when first presented by ancient Greece - just consider replacing a shepherd boy with someone spreading fake news on social media and the same story would still resonate deeply!

"The Ant and the Grasshopper" by Aesop can be an eye-opener! Not only is this tale about hard work and preparation; it's also a commentary on social responsibility and individual choice - as evidenced by how diligent ants store up food for winter while their counterpart grasshopper is preoccupied with singing and dancing and finds himself destitute when cold sets in. Some might view Aesop's story as offering us an idealized hero; yet others argue it subtly questions the notion of societies where some individuals thrive while others languish; see Aesop? Layered complexity at its finest!

Diving deeper, we should explore the linguistic genius of Aesop's fables. He not only packed them full of wisdom; he was also adept at crafting short yet memorable morals that serve as shorthand for complex ideas that are easily shared among society. Aesop created unforgettable morals like "Honesty is the best policy" and "Look before you leap", becoming part of everyday speech thanks to Aesop. These succinct morals serve as shorthand for complex ideas which are easily shared and digested by society at large - much thanks to Aesop!

But these timeless tales don't stay put: they remain alive. Over the centuries, Aesop's tales have been transformed into plays, operas, ballets and blockbuster movies; each adaptation adds its own layer of charm while maintaining Aesop's core message: some truths remain timeless! That is one of Aesop's great achievements - his wisdom lives on through successive adaptations!

Remember the cultural journey these fables have undergone. Aesop's wisdom has traveled across civilizations from its Roman adaptation by Phaedrus to Ibn al-Muqaffa's incorporation of it in Islamic folklore to becoming children's stories across the globe - sparking interesting discussions about fluidity and adaptability in wisdom tales. This, my friends, opens up an engaging discussion on this fascinating topic!

Book 2: Norse Mythology

2.1 Odin's Wisdom and Thor's Might: The Divine Inhabitants of Asgard

Welcome to the frosty realms of Norse mythology, where gods and goddesses reside within Asgard - their celestial fortress containing divine inhabitants of both wisdom and power. If Greek mythology was an adventure, just wait till you see Norse myths! They offer even greater intensity with Odin the Allfather clashing with Thor, his son with unbridled power and wild passions. This divine father-son duo forms an auspicious cosmos that not only rules over heaven and Earth, but also influences human fates and nature itself. There's an entire cast of characters we should get acquainted with; for now let's focus on two iconic figures - Odin with his two ravens Huginn and Muninn who serve as his eyes and ears in the world; and Thor, the thunder god known for wielding Mjolnir as his weapon.

Odin is a complicated figure. He doesn't just sit around Asgard doling out bits of wisdom like it's no big deal; nope; instead he is on an endless quest for knowledge and insight that has seen him sacrifice an eye at Mimir's well for just one sip of cosmic wisdom! Yet his thirst remains undiminished; it extends well beyond Asgard to humanity itself as well as into the depths of

Hell itself! Wisdom serves him like no sword or spear could: equipping him to stave off Ragnarok--the end of this world as well! No kidding: this guy really is saving our world-saving wisdom!

But let's not overlook Thor. While Odin symbolizes wisdom and rulership, Thor stands for bravery and physical might - two simple virtues which go together beautifully. Before you think Thor is just all muscle without brains, consider this: his might isn't only used for squashing giants or fighting serpents - his strength acts as a protective measure to defend Asgard and, by extension, the entire universe. Think of him like the large security guard at an ancient palace who wields an energy source capable of both creation and destruction simultaneously!

So, as we can see, Odin and Thor are two sides of one ancient Norse coin - integral parts of cosmic order. Each represents an aspect of divine power that impacts daily lives and moral landscapes for humans and other beings alike. They're not simply characters in stories; they represent powerful archetypes that still resonate today.

Before we continue, let us make one thing clear: While Odin and Thor may dominate headlines, Asgard contains an entire divine cast which deserves equal credit. Of course, we have only just scratched the surface - there are numerous gods and goddesses waiting to be discovered who each possess unique roles, powers, and stories.

As we explore further, it's crucial to keep in mind that Odin and Thor are but two vibrant personalities in Asgard; they are part of an intricate celestial community filled with relationships spanning alliances, rivalries, romances, and marital affairs that echo throughout the Nine Worlds like an ever-evolving soap opera written by cosmic scriptwriters. Odin himself has Frigg as his spouse - not simply as background character but a goddess herself with powers rivaling Odin's; her presence adds emotional complexity into what otherwise austere halls as Valhalla might otherwise lack.

Thor's relationship with his half-brother Loki, the trickster god, is no less complex. You might mistake Thor's hammer as being solely used to smash stuff, but it also serves as a barrier against Loki's ceaseless schemes. Their interactions offer an engaging window into power's duality: raw strength versus cunningness or directness against subterfuge; their differing approaches to problem-solving illustrate divine beings are complex beings just like humans are.

Even as we get drawn into the interactions of these celestial VIPs, let us not lose sight of their ensemble cast. Many gods and goddesses in Asgard play important yet often overlooked roles: Freyja embodies how various experiences intersect with one another whereas Heimdall serves as the watchman of gods, providing vital protection from Ragnarok when it begins knocking at Asgard's doors. His role might seem passive at first glance but you'll thank me when that door closes behind you!

Each god and goddess adds their own distinctive touch to Norse mythology, adding depth and variety. Understanding their individual attributes and relationships deepens our comprehension of this grand cosmic architecture. While it might be easy to get distracted by more famous figures such as Odin or Thor, keep in mind that each deity plays a unique role in maintaining this intricate divine ecosystem.

But enough about Asgard's divine inhabitants already! In the next sections, we'll take a deeper dive into its cosmic architecture--namely Yggdrasil--that houses these deities as well as explore mysterious beings such as Norns who shape destiny and provide support services. Don't get us started yet- we bet it has you intrigued!

As you explore this collection of myths and legends, prepare yourself for more eye-opening revelations and riveting narratives that will keep you engaged. Norse mythology is not simply an outdated relic from history; rather it remains relevant today, inspiring and challenging us to look beyond our immediate realities and into an infinite variety of possibilities. Are you ready to navigate its labyrinthine depths of divine intricacies and cosmic wonders? Then let's turn the page!

2.2.1 Who Was Odin and What Did He Seek?

Odin, a mysterious seeker with only one eye and god who's often shrouded in mystery and paradoxes, stands out as an intriguing figure who sought knowledge at any cost - no pun intended! Right from the get go it should be made clear that Odin wasn't your typical arm-wrestling beer-chugging deity but more like an intellectual philosopher god with an insatiable desire for wisdom that led him to sacrifice one eye at Mimir's Well just so he could drink from its wisdom-infused waters - but don't go just yet; keep reading because you will get more details!

Odin, or Allfather in Norse mythology, plays the central role in life creation and maintenance. His influence extends far and wide--from war and death to poetry and magic--everything from war and death to poetry and magic! Odin wore many hats. For instance, his pursuit of wisdom led him to mastering runic alphabet symbols used for healing wounds or changing weather; all without using academic theory! Nor did his wisdom go unused--his advice had real-life applications!

He was the ultimate strategist. His wisdom wasn't simply passive: it was actionable wisdom that helped Vikings make informed decisions during sea voyages and raids. Odin's dual nature epitomizes Norse culture: both strength and knowledge were valued equally in their cultural ethos; both were respected.

Odin's exploits went beyond battle planning and rune crafting; his ambitions extended into uncovering the mysteries of life and death, leading him on an ultimate spiritual adventure to Hel (Norse Underworld) not for casual visits but in order to speak to spirits for insights into afterlife and future. One could describe him as an unparalleled spiritual explorer keen on charting both Midgard (human world) and Hel as spiritual worlds.

Why did Odin seek knowledge across so many fields with such intensity? His motivation may lie in his preoccupation with Ragnarok, Norse mythology's version of apocalypse. Odin understood this catastrophic event was inevitable and that his death would occur during this cosmic battle; his wisdom-seeking was therefore focused on understanding it, preparing for it and making sure a new world survived post-apocalypse.

He is not simply a one-dimensional character; he's an intricate, multifaceted god who personified the intellectual and spiritual yearnings that were central to Norse culture. His thirst for knowledge not only made him one of Norse mythology's polymath gods but also created an intriguing figure who remains deeply embedded into Norse lore today. As you explore his more mysterious character in subsequent parts of this segment, more layers will reveal themselves that deepen his complexity even further; strap in and get ready! It will be exciting!

His presence can be felt throughout the Nine Worlds and vice versa. He plays an essential part in the existence of Yggdrasil, the World Tree; not just as its creator but as part of its ongoing existence as well. This symbolic representation serves to represent everything around him in some way; one way this manifests is through runes carved onto its trunk that offer power and insight if one understands their significance.

Odin is truly captivating because, despite his cosmic power and wisdom, he's not an infallible god. His flaws rival those of any god in terms of magnitude. He tends to become deeply introspective - sometimes to the point of brooding - while his obsession with Ragnarok can cause him to make morally dubious choices. Odin serves as a reminder that even gods are human too and wisdom doesn't always equal righteousness.

Odin's impact can also be felt throughout daily life in the Viking Age. People invoked him for everything from successful raids to safe voyages; people would also carry around images of him to invoke his favor and invoke him through oral storytelling tradition of Norse people; through epic tales and songs they passed along his wisdom, follies, and complexity as part of oral storytelling tradition thus cementing him into everyday culture even today.

He represents all these various qualities at once and they come together into an intriguing whole: Odin represents our pursuit of knowledge, our willingness to pay any price for wisdom, and facing unavoidable destiny without retreat. He shows us that even in a world destined to destruction, knowledge is still the highest calling and pursuit thereof should remain the highest calling.

Odin remains a compelling figure in our collective imagination for good reason: He captures humanity's struggle with mortality, the quest for wisdom and the difficulty associated with balancing morality with necessity in an attractive yet relatable form. Even after thousands of years have passed since Viking ships sailed around him.

2.1.2 Thor, the Thunder God: More than Just a Hammer

If you think Thor is simply known for wielding Mjolnir as his signature weapon, prepare yourself for an exhilarating journey of discovery! Let us show you just why Mjolnir can be seen as more than that!

Make no mistake: Thor is more than the Norse equivalent of bodybuilder with a sledgehammer. Born to Odin and Frigg, Thor is a deity with deep symbolism representing our connection to nature: earth, sky, forces of nature etc. He serves as protector to both gods and humans - something Odin himself often shies away from.

Tanngrisnir and Tanngnjostr goats don't just serve as Thor's transportation; they represent his connection to common folk, agriculture, and pastoral life - making up an integral part of his character, just like his mighty hammer is to Odin. You could say these goats represent something so fundamental to Thor that they almost seem to define him!

Let's discuss Thor's iconic hammer, Mjolnir. Most people see it as an instrument of destruction (and it certainly can be), but its soft side was often underestimated - for example it was often used during rituals to bless marriages, births and funerals and reveal another side to Thor that often gets obscured by his warrior image.

Don't misunderstand. Thor was a warrior through and through, his hammer representing nature's destructive forces such as thunderbolts, lightning storms and other natural events; yet at the same time it served as an instrument of creation and nurture - much like rainwater does for soil health - thus emphasizing his multidimensional personality as both deity and mortal figure with duties spanning both heavens and Earth.

Thor was both charming and terrifying in his personality. With a laugh that could send shockwaves through Asgard, and an impassive nature that could cause cataclysmic battles to ensue. Thor symbolized all human emotions on an extreme scale.

Let us not overlook Thor's relationships with women, particularly Sif, his wife and goddess of fertility and family life. She is famous for her golden locks which represent fields of wheat. Together they strengthen his connection to Earth and domestic life as he further cements it through their union.

Let's talk more about Loki. While you may know of his brotherly rivalry with Thor, their relationship was more like frenemies on a cosmic level. Loki's knack for chaos often put him at odds with Thor while they shared in numerous adventures together - their relationship represents an ongoing balance between order and chaos.

Thor was not only protected and led in battle by Loki; his community included Heimdall and Valhalla's brave warriors as well. This reinforced Thor's role as protector and leader, in contrast to Odin who preferred contemplative reflection over military conflict.

Thor was not just known for partying with gods and vanquishing giants; he also had an affinity for humanity as the "Everyman's God", making himself easily approachable and approachable for most. People would pray to Thor for good weather or protection during journeys or for strength to endure daily struggles.

Let us not overlook how Thor has been reimagined over time, from ancient sagas to comic books and movies. Although these adaptations offer unique and often entertaining interpretations of his character, they rarely capture all his complexity; more often than not he becomes simplified into an archetypal depiction of brute strength that belittles his complex mythic origins.

Thor's mythos is an allegory for human experience. His myth encapsulates our fascination with nature's wild forces while representing our desire for protection and strength - as well as showing our vulnerabilities. By understanding Thor, you're not simply learning about an old god from an ancient pantheon - rather, you are engaging with a character study of mankind as a whole.

2.1.3 Freyja, Loki, and Other Notable Aesir and Vanir

While Odin and Thor may dominate Norse mythology, but to fully appreciate its traditions it would be unwise not to acknowledge other divine beings within the Aesir and Vanir tribes of gods. Freyja, the goddess of love, beauty, and war is an indispensable character who transcends her singular role. Not only is she revered as the embodiment of feminine beauty and femininity; she's also an impressive warrior capable of pulling a powerful chariot pulled by cats (yes! cats!). Folkvangr, which she presides over as an afterlife realm. Half of those who die in battle enter its halls. With an intense depth of character combining strength and vulnerability that has inspired numerous legends and epics.

Loki, the god of mischief and one of the most intriguing figures in all of Norse mythology, can often be an unpredictable presence. One never really knows what's going on behind his crafty mind; is he friendly towards Aesir or harmful? But the truth lies somewhere between - Loki has been described as being someone who gets you into trouble but will also help get out of it--mostly. His unpredictable actions throughout sagas force one to reconsider morality itself - that's the beauty of Loki; not everything fits neatly; forcing us all to confront murky depths between right and wrong complexities - which he does brilliantly.

But it isn't all gods and goddesses; the Vanir, often considered "the other tribe," also bring their own perspectives and influences into play. While Aesir are more commonly associated with warfare and rulership, Vanir are deities associated with fertility, prosperity and nature; Njord, Freyr and Freyja being key figures among them who represent natural resources on land and sea. So influential were they that after an Aesir-Vanir war was concluded they agreed upon an exchange of hostages to maintain peace, effectively merging both forces while merging their strengths into one uniting strength while effectively merging their strengths as well as influence spheres.

Not to be outdone by their counterparts in Norse mythology, we cannot ignore the roles played by other important beings such as Valkyries, Norns, and Jotunn. Valkyries serve Odin by selecting only brave warriors killed during battle to enter Valhalla - making them as integral to Norse afterlife concepts as any god or goddess. Norns are seen as analogous to Greek Fates (Fates in Latin mythology), controlling both gods and mortals' fates while their morality remains somewhat questionable than Loki; nonetheless their mysteriousness leaves room for wonderment and speculation. Jotunns play their own unique roles within mythological myths by virtue of being.

Plunging deeper into these entities not only expands our view of Norse cosmology but also deepens our understanding of how Norse people perceived the world. A nuanced spectrum of divine morality and influence emerges, forcing us to question more deeply our cultural and spiritual assumptions. When we explore these lesser-known yet profoundly influential characters we're doing more than filling gaps; rather we're expanding horizons, opening ourselves up to an appreciation of Norse mythology's lush tapestry of complex fabric.

But let's talk about other gods from this intriguing Norse pantheon! Freyr, Freyja's brother and leader among the Vanir, represents abundance in harvest and peace. While you might view him as peaceful, make no mistake: when push comes to shove he is just as powerful a fighter than any other god; remember he gave away his sword just so he could win over Giantess Freyja? Nevertheless, even without it, Freyr is expected to hold his own in Ragnarok at its conclusion - talk about multidimensional personalities!

Oh and how could we forget Balder, the beloved Aesir god? Known for his unparalleled beauty and wisdom, Balder seems too good to be true; yet his tragic demise at Loki's hands remains one of the most poignant tales from Norse epics. While Balder lived a full life filled with light, his sudden departure casts a dark shadow which portends events leading up to Ragnarok. Balder encapsulates Norse acceptance of both happiness and sorrow that life presents us.

And let's not limit our exploration to deities alone: Jotunn - often depicted as giants and foes of the gods - play an integral part in Norse cosmology as well. But these Jotunn are more than simple antagonists: Skadi is an example of one who became part of Aesir and represents winter's harshness while embodying resilience and independence; many gods like Odin and Thor even possess Jotunn blood within them! Talk about a complicated family tree!

Never could we close without giving due recognition to the animal companions of the gods - legends in their own right! From Odin's ravens, Huginn and Muninn, which traveled all around to bring news back home to him; Freyja's cat-driven chariot; Thor's indomitable goats Tanngrisnir and Tanngnjostr; these legendary companions add depth and relatability to the divine figures they serve.

By exploring these fascinating characters in-depth, we go beyond simply collecting myths or understanding a religious practice; instead we connect to the core of human thought itself. Norse deities, goddesses, and beings act as mirrors to our own beliefs, virtues, and flaws. By playing out various aspects of human experience in miniature on an eternal stage - love, hate, jealousy, joy, sorrow - they offer an insight into the human psyche that makes us reflect upon ourselves more closely and identify areas for improvement in ourselves and society as whole. No more thrilling way exists to appreciate the timeless wisdom of Norse mythology than through music and dance! Every tale serves as a mirror reflecting our human condition - we have only just scratched the surface! So hold tight, as this journey through Norse mythology only just begins.

2.1.4 The Bifrost Bridge and Cosmic Architecture

At first glance, it may look like just another stunning rainbow bridge from modern popular culture; but I assure you, the Bifrost Bridge in Norse mythology serves more than merely aesthetic purpose: it connects Asgard (the realm of gods) to Midgard (our world) via Asgard Bridge. But its purpose goes much deeper; Norse mythology uses Bifrost Bridge as a remarkable metaphor representing divine connection, impermanence and reaching towards cosmos!

The Bifrost is often imagined as an ethereal structure. Protected by Heimdallr - who can hear grass grow and see hundreds of miles - this bridge serves as an important cosmic checkpoint. Only gods and those they designate may traverse it, making it sacred space. But why even create such an elaborate bridge in the first place? Because its symbolic value suggests that gods and humans share one multiverse.

At its core, the Bifrost contributes to Norse mythology's complex Nine Worlds architecture. These interlinked realms don't exist as distinct entities floating aimlessly; instead they mirror our own ecosystem in their interactions between realms. Yggdrasil serves as another central pillar in this architecture with roots reaching across each realm - while Bifrost provides direct but controlled interaction between divine and mundane realms - echoing Norse cosmology's theme of interconnectivity.

And while discussing Yggdrasil, let us not underestimate its connection with Bifrost. When contemplating Ragnarok looms closer, both cosmic tree Yggdrasil and its bridge Bifrost seem to tremble simultaneously--reminding us all of their humanity and fragility. Yet Bifrost stands as an indication of both physical fragility and moral/ethical frailty, setting up one of Norse myth's most poignant scenes--gods crossing to meet their fate during Ragnarok--this bridge understands its dual role of serving both divine glory and divine folly simultaneously!

The Bifrost plays an integral part in Norse perceptions of color, light and materiality. It often appears in depictions as rainbows--an ephemeral phenomenon which captured Vikings' fascination with fleeting beauty--while also providing a fantastical blend of earth, water, fire and air elements whose existence cannot be quantified easily or categorized firmly enough for easy categorization. Its ever-shifting hues may represent gods themselves or simply wind off the

North Sea--winds which always change at their discretion!

Another intriguing element of the bridge's semi-permeable nature is its selectivity; not everyone is allowed to cross. This suggests an element of the divine screening process and reinforces the concept that reaching gods requires more than physical journeying; reaching them requires spiritual selection as well. Perhaps this early form of worthiness theory that has persisted throughout religions could provide some clues. So are you worthy enough to walk the same path as gods?

Before we go off in an abstract philosophical direction, let's bring this back down to earth by considering how richly this adds narratively to Norse myths. Imagine all the drama, emotional highs and lows and sheer existential curiosity the Bifrost awakens within those who hear its tales; whether Thor is thundering across it to stop some mischief-making giant or gods crossing solemnly on their way towards Ragnarok; this stage provides some of the most riveting dramas from Norse mythology!

What happens to The Bifrost as a character, not simply as an object or backdrop? Just as any worthwhile story follows its protagonist through change and growth, sometimes with disastrous ends; so too does The Bifrost come full circle when its destruction during

Ragnarok becomes emotionally charged as any hero or deity's downfall; its collapse not only takes an era with it; it signifies profound cosmic shifts.

Think for a second about what a broken bridge means in mythological terms: not getting from A to B is no big deal in reality; but in mythological terms, a collapsed bridge represents chaos, disconnection from divinity, and forceful passage into new states of being. A collapsed bridge doesn't just signal infrastructure failure; rather, it represents a spiritual crisis akin to human isolation from things greater than ourselves; even gods must recognize their mortality through breaking links that once represented limitless existence - something symbolized by breaking off rainbow links which once represented hope ethereally rainbow links before collapsing.

Norse mythology's bridge-breaking moment marks a crucial transition for every element, not simply as one event but as an ever-evolving process. It signals the decline of gods, the reconfiguration of realms, and even a possible birth from sea's murky depths of an entirely new universe arising out of chaos and death. Norse cosmology emphasizes cyclical existence: death and rebirth: it doesn't just provide pure doom but an opportunity for transformation; much like any character facing a tragic end, Bifrost leaves behind an imprint on the mythological landscape with which it is connected.

Legacy aside, Bifrost can be found echoed across other cultural narratives and practices. Take Celtic and Saxon mythologies which feature similar bridges or pathways between realms; while not identical these structures often serve as thresholds with transformative potential; not to mention Eastern philosophy where transcending ignorance into enlightenment is central theme - suggesting people from diverse times and cultures share an inherent fascination for divine or cosmic pathways.

Why is Bifrost still relevant today? Because its existence serves as an illustration of life's transience and the perpetual tension between mundane existence and spiritual spirituality. While we may not experience physical rainbow bridges in our daily lives, thresholds can still provide opportunities to challenge beliefs or enter unfamiliar territories that offer both opportunities and threats - like Bifrost itself.

And as we stand on the brink of life-altering decisions, perhaps we can draw inspiration from Norse gods: even in times of inevitable decline there can still be room for courage and choices that shape the narratives of our personal histories. If an inanimate bridge can personify such profound themes while stirring existential inquiry, imagine what you as a complex human can signify in your personal story?

2.2 The Doom of Gods: Ragnarok and the Norse Apocalypse

Every epic tale has its highs and lows, but something particularly captivating about its climax stands out. Such is the case of Norse mythology's grand finale-- Ragnarok. Marvel may make shows about end times; Ragnarok takes that idea one step further with its intricate, inevitable dance of destruction and renewal that has puzzled philosophers and scholars for generations.

Let's ease into this by first asking: what exactly is Ragnarok? While it might be tempting to view Ragnarok simply as an end of all things scenario, you would miss out on its nuanced tapestry that makes it much more than an Armageddon equivalent. In Old Norse, Ragnarok roughly translates as 'Fate of the Gods,' an expression with profound philosophical implications; you see, Ragnarok isn't simply an event but instead represents an entire Norse worldview that gives us insight into their spiritual and moral compass encapsulating humanity alike.

Ragnarok represents the Viking belief in time's circular nature. Time doesn't progress linearly from point A to B; rather it moves in circles; or, to be precise, an intricate web of loops and twists leading back around until eventually coming full circle again. Not to forget this loop either! Ragnarok is more than an end of life on Earth; rather it serves as cosmic purification that ushers in a new age with renewed hope of brighter times ahead.

So where does this grand narrative begin? It starts with an array of omens and signs, sending shockwaves across the realms and setting the scene for what is to come - cosmic winters, solar eclipses, natural disasters and war and chaos among humankind all feature as significant events; animal kingdom is even given a heads-up - with howling wolves howling and birds chirping as though sensing something dire! However don't be scared off; this prelude offers ample time for both gods- and us- to come to terms with our fateful destiny!

Although this epic tale features epic battles, fire giants, and monstrosities of every variety, its moral and existential undercurrents go well beyond what its action sequences might initially suggest. Each god meets their fate with poetic justice as both their strengths and flaws come to fruition in character arcs such as Odin the Allfather of Aesir's quest for knowledge and power concludes in a confrontation with cosmic wolf Jormungandr (The Midgard Serpent). Or Thor who faces off against Jormungandr (The Midgard Serpent).

2.2.1 The Prophecy of Ragnarok: A Foretold End

Prophecies are at the core of any epic tale, and in Ragnarok they provide us with an intriguing lens through which to examine its unfolding events. Not just vague sayings or verses either: Norse poets left us an entire ancient poetic manuscript known as Voluspa that served as the ultimate handbook for an apocalyptic disaster written as part of Poetic Edda; written as this text reads like an ultimate spoiler alert without much chance to avert it before its arrival! But before delving deeper, let's examine how this prophecy came into being.

Odin, the god of wisdom, feels his thirst for knowledge increasing with each passing day. Unsolved cosmic riddles seem endlessly puzzling him; so, to satisfy this insatiable thirst he turns to divination, which in Norse culture was closely associated with female shamans known as volvas. Odin decides to summon one from her grave so he may question her about past, present, and future events using magic and ritual - the Voluspa is born!

Prophecy begins by offering an idyllic vision of the universe, from creation myths to early age gods and giants. It tells of Yggdrasil as an essential world tree holding all creation together as well as Norns - fates responsible for shaping gods as well as men's fates -

who shape our destinies through destiny-giving fates that shape each life as its fate is written out. Don't be misled by its seemingly serene setup; the real meat of the prophecy begins to come forth when a volva begins describing events leading up to Ragnarok. According to her, Fimbulvetr will bring three years of extreme, merciless winter, making regular winters look like tropical vacations in comparison. However, this winter serves a greater purpose; it represents how the universe's gears are shifting towards its end times.

But, what of the gods themselves? Their fates are also set out with great precision; almost as though their script were written for them. Odin must battle Fenrir, an enormous monstrous wolf; Thor must battle Midgard Serpent; Freyja must meet Surt, the fire giant; each battle not just a clash but rather an expression of character destiny, reflecting virtues, vices and key roles each god plays in cosmic drama.

There's drama to be found in how the gods react to this revelation of their fates. Knowing your destiny is one thing; accepting it is another entirely. But it would be inaccurate to view them as passive recipients of fate; quite the contrary! They take an active, and aggressive, role in seeking knowledge and preparing for what lies ahead; Odin doesn't just sit passively on his celestial throne moping about impending doom; rather he actively pursues wisdom - even if that means sacrificing an eye or hanging himself from Yggdrasil;

Thor continues defending Asgard and Midgard from giants as though each victory might somehow alter its course of fate.

Just when it seems as though all is lost - gods have met their tragic ends, and the world is in smoldering ruins--the Voluspa reveals another twist in its tale. Following Ragnarok, Voluspa tells of what comes after: not an endless void but instead, after cosmic turmoil has subsided, an entirely new world emerges from beneath its waters; fertile and fresh like an ultimate reboot for our universe. Keep this thought in mind; its significance extends not just for understanding Norse myths but also for its deeper philosophy within its mythos story itself.

We tend to dwell too much on destruction that we neglect this essential aspect of renewal - an essential balance to its destructive power. The Norse in their wisdom understood this cycle well enough; even their divine order wasn't immortal and must eventually succumb to life, death and rebirth--cyclicality at its finest! While the old world may be gone forevermore, its legacy provides space for a brand new one with none of its former flaws or gods remaining; paradoxically providing comforting assurance that endings don't spell doom; rather they lead onward into fresh new beginnings!

There's an amazing moment in The Voluspa wherein Odin's two sons, Vidar and Vali, inherit his throne while Thor's Modi and Magni take ownership of Mjolnir - two symbolic and poetic gestures which mirror both deeds and virtues from previous kings while offering something new and unexplored - it makes sense that this prophecy would prompt us to think about legacy: how can one honor both past and present while encouraging the development of future generations? Not just gods but all mortals should reflect upon this question as it pertains to us mortals too!

Voluspa's Voluspa manuscript provides another eye-opener: it doesn't merely focus on gods alone. Instead, it briefly touches upon human survival and renewal: Lif and Lifthrasir are human survivors who hide within Yggdrasil during Ragnarok and later return to populate Earth afterward. This short glimpse at humanity serves as a grounding factor; reminding us that godly drama doesn't happen in isolation but has ripple effects across realms, affecting even those most mundane beings.

So as we make sense of the complexity and nuances of Ragnarok prophecy, let us not lose sight of its nuance: this prophecy serves as a poignant testament to Norse understanding of a universe bound by fate yet offering new beginnings and opportunities for hope.

Prophecies provide us with an object lesson in humility by showing even gods they're not immune from nature's cycles that govern all existence, such as natural cycles and fate. They show how hubris cannot outwit fate - yet all along there remains an everlasting promise of renewal within its lines, reminding us there will always be another dawn waiting with new tales and truths for us to explore.

2.2.2 The Role of Jormungandr, the World Serpent

First, let's set some context. Jormungandr is one of three monstrous children conceived from Loki and Angrboda; due to this relationship he's unlikely to end up as an ordinary cubicle dweller; nope, Jormungandr's destiny was always set aside as part of cosmic events and decided that its best home was the ocean that surrounds Midgard, human world. There, Jormungandr became so enormous he could wrap around Earth, encircling Earth twice before grasping his tail in his mouth; acting like a living, breathing fence that demarcates known world boundaries from each other hex- helix.

Are we on board yet? Excellent! Because understanding Jormungandr's role in Ragnarok means understanding his symbolic representation as a representation of destructive forces lurking on the edges of our existence, always ready to wreak havoc upon it all. He stands as not just another monster but instead represents a fearful unknown that can bring chaos with its chaos-wrecking rampages - quite an intimidating role for one creature, even one as vast as World Serpent!

So how does Jormungandr figure into Ragnarok, you ask? Simply this: when the end of the world begins, Jormungandr lets go of his tail and uncoils, dismantling barriers against chaos. While this might not sound significant at first, its significance lies deeper: this action not only signals its beginning; it contributes directly to unraveling Earth itself - oceans rise, land floods, natural laws change... It's as though Jormungandr is acting like an alarm clock - everyone involved must wake up and brace themselves accordingly.

Just when you think his role has ended, the serpent-like monster steps forward for an epic showdown: Thor, the God of Thunder. Yes, this showdown is not only monumental and symbolic - Thor as champion of order and protector of his realms must confront one of its epitome. Before, these two had already had some skirmishes but now there is one final showdown, an ultimate clash for history's record books.

The tragedy lies in both Thor and Jormungandr's failure to emerge victorious in an absolute sense. While Thor succeeds in killing Jormungandr, he succumbs to its deadly venom shortly thereafter and dies shortly afterwards - serving as a reminder that even in victory the forces of order cannot escape chaos's forces; defeat of Jormungandr comes at great cost - symbolizing both sacrifice and triumph against overwhelming odds.

This theme goes far beyond simple Norse fatalism: it encapsulates an important philosophical understanding of life itself. Struggles are inevitable and victories often bring their own set of losses; therefore this tale asks us to consider: Are we prepared to sacrifice something for order and stability, or can there be room for reconciliation against chaotic forces?

Jormungandr's myth can be read as an examination of how opposing forces interact. Strangely enough, World Serpent and Thor rely on each other; their roles define each other yet remain irrevocably linked - an essential cycle that keeps balance in our universe.

Be mindful that Jormungandr is the product of Loki, the god of mischief and change. Like his father, Jormungandr embodies aspects that are both frightening and necessary; unlike pure evil beings like Loki he represents natural forces that, while frightening at first sight, are essential components of our world's fabric. Through understanding Jormungandr we must confront uncomfortable truths such as creation and destruction being twin sides of an intricate dance between one another.

Jormungandr isn't simply an invention of Norse imagination - the serpent is an universal symbol and can be found throughout many mythologies around the world. Yet its role in Norse tales stands apart, providing us with fresh perspectives on themes like death, renewal, and time's cycle.

Let's first address Ouroboros, the ancient symbol of a serpent eating its own tail. Known by Greeks, but found all around the world in mythologies from Egyptian to Indian traditions - This image symbolizes life's endless cycle - birth, death and rebirth with no beginning or end point in sight. If Jormungandr releases his tail during Ragnarok does that mean breaking Ouroboros?

Well, not necessarily. While the World Serpent's act may cause chaos to ensue, its actions shouldn't be seen as the end of anything but as necessary disruption that leads to renewal. Sometimes you must break things in order to create something.

Now let's consider how Jormungandr has permeated modern thought. Carl Jung, the Swiss psychiatrist who pioneered the collective unconscious concept, saw serpents as symbols of transformation. According to Jungian psychology, facing our inner serpent is essential for personal development - we must face our deepest fears, most unsettling thoughts in order to become whole individuals again. Thor's fight with Jormungandr can serve as an external representation of this psychological struggle within.

It's fascinating that the World Serpent has found its way into pop culture. Be it movies or video games, references to cataclysmic snakes often recall ancient mythology and carry symbols associated with chaos and renewal - as though Jormungandr had somehow embedded itself within our collective storytelling - reminding us to maintain equilibrium between order and chaos, destruction and renewal.

But what are the practical ramifications of this myth, you ask? Consider this: as our planet becomes ever more vulnerable to existential threats such as climate change, political turmoil or pandemics--Jormungandr's story serves as a cautionary tale and reminder that forces we disregard or underestimate may well become threats in themselves; much as Jormungandr was underestimated until it was too late; similarly we could underestimate threats on the horizon just like they underestimated Jormungandr.

At the same time, Thor's tale promotes resilience. Thor is aware that his battle with the serpent will likely end his life; nonetheless he goes forward and fights anyway; an inspiring example of facing challenges head-on even when odds seem overwhelming; his sacrifice ultimately led to new beginnings for all involved; it serves as both hope and cautionary tale with its message of courage and perseverance embodied by Thor.

2.2.3 How Ragnarok Influences Norse Ethics and Morality

Are You Captivated By Ragnarok's Plotline, Eh? Believe me, there's more to Ragnarok than just its end-of-world catastrophes and cosmic battles. This apocalyptic tale had a significant influence on Norse people's ethics and morality beliefs - you might even find out that Ragnarok wasn't just an action-packed blockbuster of gods but served as a moral guideline for society as well! So buckle up as we go deeper!

Let me start off by making it clear: the concept of an apocalypse in Norse mythology differs considerably from other religious or mythological traditions. Instead of serving as a "judgment day" that separates good from bad people, Ragnarok acts more like an universal reset button that neither gods nor mortals can escape; its neutrality being an important symbolism on ethics-- implying that nature does not hold favoritism over human and divine actions alike.

Here, the focus is not a system of rewards and punishments but instead on life itself: life, death, and rebirth. Even gods like Odin and Thor, who embody specific virtues like wisdom and courage respectively, come to an end eventually. Although this might initially appear depressing or hopeless, this understanding can actually be liberating: since even gods cannot escape their fates, then what matters more than end results is actually journeys taken and actions undertaken that reflect ethical considerations; placing emphasis firmly on principles by which one lives life.

At its heart, Norse society valued virtues like bravery, loyalty and honor not just as lofty ideals but pragmatic necessities. Their harsh environmental conditions - long winters with scant resources- required community cooperation for survival; you had to be brave when confronting real physical challenges; you must remain loyal and honorable because your community depended on it - in this sense the harshness and unpredictability of life reflected the gods they worshiped and their volatile universe in which these gods existed.

Speaking of which, "wyrd," or fate, played an essential role here. Wyrd wasn't simply predetermined but an ever-evolving weave influenced by individual actions - although Ragnarok was inevitable for everyone, you had control over which threads you contributed to reality; thus morality became an active process through which decisions made would shape both individual fate as well as collective destiny.

Let's consider "drengskapr," the Norse code of chivalry that stressed courage, honor and justice. Drengskapr wasn't limited to warriors - it influenced society as a whole as well. Take, for instance, Iceland's Althing parliament; one of its oldest parliaments that upheld legal judgments that were heavily influenced by this code of ethics that in turn was informed by wider cosmological theories such as Ragnarok.

At the dawn of an imminent end, virtues gained greater significance. If our universe were to end one day and start over, maintaining honor and fulfilling duties became existential imperatives rather than mere expectations; acting virtuously wasn't done just to avoid posthumous punishment but to create a healthy society in a microcosmic universe itself.

Norse sagas have long been considered morality plays. Their central characters face impossible ethical decisions that inevitably result in tragedy or loss - take the Volsunga Saga for instance: its characters often find themselves facing morally compromised situations that test their mettle - giving insight into Norse understandings of right and wrong, good and evil.

Sigurd kills Fafnir not for gold or glory but to fulfill an inherent sense of destiny akin to Ragnarok; yet his actions create a tragic chain reaction which takes everyone involved by surprise and results in their deaths; serving as an examination of our actions no matter how noble.

Ragnarok provides the backdrop to all these stories and ethical quandaries, serving as the ever-present reminder that time is fleeting and actions have consequences that ripple out into wyrd. It serves as an object lesson of humility; reminding us all that no matter our grand ambitions or heroic deeds, we're part of an unpredictable narrative we can influence but never fully control - perhaps this lesson should serve as our greatest moral lesson of all.

2.2.4 Rebirth and Renewal: Life After the Apocalypse

Once Ragnarok has ended and all is destroyed by its chaos and fires, what remains? It can be easy to become overwhelmed by destruction and overlook one crucial component of the Norse apocalypse: renewal. Not just an end; Ragnarok marks a new start: it is a cosmic reset button which sets things right again! But don't take this to be some simplistic silver lining; rather it provides fascinating insights into Norse cosmology that gives this ancient society view cycles--of nature as well as human endeavor and cosmic cycles--in terms.

At its core, Norse worldview is circular rather than linear: seasons come and go, lives are lived and lost, even gods undergo cycles of death and rebirth; recall how Odin gained wisdom by offering up an eye at Mimir's well and hanging himself from Yggdrasil, the world tree; it represents death as a form of transformation in order to return as god of wisdom - so when talking about Ragnarok we shouldn't think of it simply as the final curtain call but as a transitional phase within an endless cycle of cosmic events!

Rebirth after Ragnarok isn't just an abstract concept; the myths explicitly address it. A small group of gods survive, including Odin's sons Vidar and Vali and Thor's Modi and Magni, to find themselves living in a world reborn - one where life seems eager to begin again; Balder's return from death as ruler shows just that resilience of life and indefatigable Norse spirit!

At first glance, it may be tempting to view this scenario as simply another "happy ending", but let us remember the serious consequences of such a fight: those who survived endure emotional and physical injuries from battle; moreover, the world they inherit has changed significantly from that which they had before the conflict; it needs rebuilding entirely from scratch - yet in doing so the gods and humanity find purpose again; the process renewing not just physical structures but also hope and the values which make life worth living.

Renewal is not exclusive to Norse mythology; it exists across different mythologies and religions as well. Hinduism features Yugas, periods that begin pure but devolve into corruption until being reset by Vishnu; even Christians believe there will be an afterlife and paradise after Judgment Day; yet Norse mythology seems less concerned with divine punishment and more on an organic cycle that includes both decay and renewal.

Ethical and moral frameworks discussed in the previous section can also undergo periodic renewal. After Ragnarok has been completely destroyed, we begin again from scratch to revise moral codes, societal norms, and personal ethics to suit a changing world with different challenges and opportunities. While values may remain the same, their application and interpretation might change to fit with these new conditions and challenges - one could argue this cyclical view of morality offers more dynamic adaptation than static laws; acknowledging impermanence while fostering adaptability and growth; essential qualities necessary to survive in an ever-evolved environment like that which exists.

How does this concept of rebirth and renewal relate to our contemporary lives? On one level, it provides us with a philosophical framework for exploring our responses to cataclysmic events - be they environmental, social or personal. When faced with our own 'Ragnarok'- a disaster, significant life change or personal loss- we may go through stages of grief, acceptance and eventual renewal; rebuilding stronger or wiser versions of ourselves much like the gods from another world would.

Norse art, literature and everyday life reflect this blueprint for new beginnings after Ragnarok. Have you heard of ouroboros--an ancient symbol depicting a serpent eating its tail--which symbolizes death and rebirth? In Norse mythology this concept symbolizes death as well as rebirth--it represents how everything begins again as we approach its end and it always returns in some shape or form--almost like tidewaters of an ocean being ever changing, just like in Norse cosmology!

Does the Norse view life with fatalistic resignation, seeing all things as eventually ending and beginning again? No. Quite the contrary: this worldview gives life an extra measure of existential responsibility: If the world and its moral and ethical frameworks are constantly shifting and reformulating, each individual has an impactful role to play in shaping its destiny; not just gods are creators or destroyers - human action contributes directly to its continued evolution and shaping of reality.

This perspective also has an enormously profound effect on how Norse approach the concept of legacy. In an endless cycle, what does it mean to leave an indelible mark? Legacy becomes something more than material accomplishments: it involves imparting wisdom, touching lives and setting an ethical and moral example that endures over time. Ragnarok and its aftermath provide immortality through impact; actions taken now could resonate in future cycles as an incredible means of leaving your mark - this may prove far more powerful than any statue or saga could.

What can we take away from all this? The notion of Ragnarok and renewal provides an inspiring narrative, simultaneously encouraging accountability and providing hope. Not just another story to entertain by the fireside; its mythic resonance resonates within human psyche to make us consider our roles within this grand, ever-renewing tapestry of existence - are we passive observers letting life shape us or do we embrace the Norse spirit of active participation by taking personal responsibility for shaping what lies before us through deeds, thoughts and values which impact far-reachful ripple effects?

Norse concepts of life after an apocalypse are both exhilarating and sobering, providing both optimism and humility in equal measures. Their vision encompasses winter's harshness with spring's revitalization; defeat's despair with its thrill of new beginning. But most significantly, their concept encapsulates what it means to be human in an unpredictable world full of gods, monsters, beauty and chaos; we are the architects of our destiny while joining an eternal dance with the universe that continues long after both us or even gods have left the stage.

2.3 Mystical Practices: Runes, Seidr, and Viking Rituals

Ragnarok has revealed to us the cosmic dimensions of Norse beliefs; now let's turn back down to earth by unraveling some of their mystifying spiritual practices - runes, seidr and various Viking rituals- to get back into reality and the here-and-now. These practices serve as spiritual tool boxes which enable individuals to interact with or make sense of our vast existence by unraveling its intricate threads! Let's untie them now?

Runes are one of the more accessible mystical elements to modern observers. Although often dismissed as simply alphabetic characters, each rune represents something much richer: symbolism packed full of meaning and energy that packs each rune like an alphanumeric letter in your name! Runes serve a similar function within Norse culture by channeling spiritual and elemental energies - not simply writing!

Runic magic may not seem as extravagant as you think it would be; no grand incantations or swirling vortices of power are involved; rather, the focus lies on inscribing runes onto objects to add special properties or serve as talismans - for instance engraving the protection rune onto your shield and believing its essence will provide protection for its bearer - this kind of thinking blurs the boundaries between mundane and mystical activities, turning everyday activities like crafting and inscribing into sacred acts that elevate mundane actions into sacred acts - creating sacred acts in this magical practice!

Now let's examine seidr, an intricate and controversial Norse mystical practice. At its core, seidr is shamanic magic rooted in Norse culture that often associated with prophecy, divination, and even will-manipulation - made most famous by Odin the Allfather who learned these arts from Freyja - not traditional magical tricks like pulling rabbits out of hats but rather altered states of consciousness achieved through singing drumming meditation or ingestion of substances- to gain insights or gain advantage for themselves or another's benefit.

Seidr was used for many different purposes - to heal or harm, to bind or release, reveal hidden truths or hide them - but it wasn't suitable for everyone - mastery required rigorous training and could lead to social consequences for men who practiced this art traditionally considered feminine; such as stigmatization for practicing male practitioners of Seidr as part of Viking society if this genre became too masculine in appearance. But let's avoid going down this rabbit hole for now.

Vikings had numerous rituals designed to ensure a good harvest or gain victory in battle, such as runes and seidr, that included ritual sacrifices known as blots (often animal offerings but sometimes human). These sacrifices were usually offered up as communal affairs involving animals but sometimes human offerings too - these sacrifices often to gods like Odin or Freyja for war, fertility or weather, Thor or Thor for weather/crops were made as community affairs to foster community relations with these deities; they weren't simply about killing an animal but rather were deeply symbolic acts meant to foster reciprocal relationships between all participants involved and gods/goddesses thereby cementing reciprocal relationships between participants and these deities as they established reciprocal relationships between humans and gods/devas or deities and humans that often existed among various communities over time.

Norse culture provides us with an insight into another way of viewing reality, where material and spiritual elements coexist as one reality. Runes, seidr and rituals reveal this as people strive for agency within an ever-expanding and unpredictable universe that seems vaster and more chaotic than themselves - such as weather conditions that either nourish or destroy crops or gods who could either protect or punish them come Ragnarok.

Think about it - these mystical practices represent a microcosm of Norse philosophy: deeply practical yet aware of something beyond our comprehension - these rituals capture the essence of a people who recognize both its wonder and danger and are ready for whatever may come their way, open to whatever comes their way with both hands on the hilt of their sword - in other words: they show who truly embrace life with both hands firmly on its hilt!

2.3.1 The Art of Runecasting: Predicting the Future

If you think fortune-telling is limited to crystal balls and tarot cards, let us expand your horizons! Yes, we will explore rune casting--an intriguing and innovative form of divination which extends the symbolic potency of runes into the realm of future prediction. Runecasting goes far beyond reading tea leaves or animal entrails (although these practices did have their place)--it involves an intricate system with philosophical overtones! So grab your cloak and shield; we are embarking upon an adventure into unknown waters!

At its core, runecasting involves tossing runes--usually carved onto pieces of wood, bone or stone--onto a surface and reading their positioning and relationships to each other. While this might sound straightforward enough, don't be fooled: each rune is more than a letter; each rune contains many hidden meanings that range from straightforward to more esoteric interpretations. In a way, each runic toss acts as a miniature version of Creation; elements are cast out into space until eventually settle meaningful patterns that reveal meaningful interpretations.

Let us elaborate. When runes are cast, their landing surface acts like a microcosm where cosmic forces come into play - this could be anything from a specially designed runic mat, animal skin or the earth; each with its own associations and implications for interpretation of runes thrown onto it. Within this universe, runes interact like celestial bodies bound by invisible laws; some might land upright while others fall face-down to signify different aspects. Others still form clusters or constellations which must be read according to what meaning each element brings out of each.

Runecasting required specific skills. A caster needed an intimate knowledge of each rune's various meanings and the wisdom to recognize more obscure or arcane interpretations depending on a question posed or situation at hand, such as when "Fehu," often associated with wealth or cattle, was adjacent to "Isa," representing standstill or ice, it may indicate your financial assets have frozen up; but context plays an essential role here, along with an intuitive reading from their ability to relate runes with larger life circumstances or cosmic events.

An additional factor that adds layers of complexity is how runes are cast; there are various methods, each providing its own lens through which to view or interpret any query or problem presented to us. One of the simplest techniques is known as the Three Norns" Spread, which draws upon Norse culture's belief in three fateful goddesses-Urd (past), Verdandi (present), and Skuld (future). To represent this practice, three runes are drawn and laid out in a row on the tabletop. The three elements represent past factors influencing a situation; current state; and a possible outcome or "window into what could yet happen". But this is just scratching the surface - more complex runic spreads such as Valknut (nine-rune layout named after Odin's symbol) provide extensive, multidimensional analysis.

Runecasting operates under the assumption that it taps into an active cosmic conversation, acting as conduits between mundane life and mysticism, providing insights that are both grounded and transcendental. A key draw of runecasting lies in its blend of fatalism and agency: While runes may reveal possible future outcomes, its very act suggests an intention to shape or alter that future by seeking knowledge about it in advance.

Now I can feel some of you raising an eyebrow in disbelief: "Isn't all of this superstitious?" If that is how you feel, keep in mind that rune casting thrived in cultures where spiritual realm was as real and tangible as wind blowing or earth shifting under foot - not because logic cannot explain everything, but because logic has limits - so let us put aside disbelief for now and explore this tantalizingly mysterious aspect of Norse spirituality together!

2.3.2 Seidr: The Ancient Practice of Norse Magic

Think dimly lit chambers filled with the aroma of burning herbs and entranced individuals swaying to an ethereal chant; that was Seidr; its power so potency even the gods themselves wouldn't dare misuse it! Volvas, predominantly women performed Seidr and were revered and respected but also deeply feared due to their abilities.

Seidr can be simply defined as an ancient form of shamanistic magic that goes far beyond spellcasting or soothsaying; its practitioners were capable of manipulating reality itself! By manipulating reality directly, these practitioners weren't simply "seeing" into other dimensions - they had influence. If that doesn't give you chills then consider yourself tough enough!

But let's peel back some layers here, shall we? Seidr is deeply embedded within Norse belief systems and to understand it fully one must first understand Yggdrasil, the World Tree with its intricate network of roots and branches that spans across Nine Worlds. Seidr was an ancient practice used for navigating these immense pathways; an early form of cosmic navigation. Practitioners would enter a trance state typically through ritualistic chanting and drumming as well as ingestion of psychoactive substances; once in this altered state they could travel along Yggdrasil's pathways to gain knowledge, wisdom, or material benefits that were tangible or not tangible at first.

Do not misconstrue this act of cosmic exploration as some reckless thrill-ride across dimensions! Navigating these cosmic pathways was fraught with danger; think of it like hacking into the source code of the universe with all of its firewalls and booby traps, risking not just metaphysical but physical harm as well as individuals failing to return from these spiritual journeys. Magic was much more serious business than what we associate it with today; it required immense skill, years of training, and an ethical compass that guided it properly.

Even within communities, Seidr was often met with fear and reverence. That was because its power could disrupt nature's balance in ways both good and evil; Seidr could bring prosperity and health but could also be used for darker endeavors like casting spells to curse an enemy's crops or, according to legends, altering fate itself woven by Norns.

Seidr is also notable for breaking ground when it comes to gender: traditionally considered feminine art form dominated by female practitioners, Seidr was revolutionary in that it gave women unrivaled power and influence at a time when this opportunity was rare. Yet Odin himself engaged in Seidr much to the disapproval of other gods and warriors who considered it "unmanly". This created a fascinating gender-fluid aspect to its practice by breaking expectations on roles typically assumed for warriors versus shield-maidens within society dominated by one versus another path; creating an intriguing gender-fluid aspect that challenges stereotypes within society where warriors and shield-maidens each had distinct paths in terms of power and influence in combat situations.

If Seidr seems like just another collection of mystifying ideas, keep your Viking helmet close because we're about to explore its fascinating interplay with social, political, and psychological facets of Norse life. Seidr wasn't simply the domain of reclusive mystics - Volvas would often be summoned to court to provide advice or predict war outcomes or intervene in social disputes - suggesting it wasn't simply an obscure practice but was actually used as an instrument of soft power that helped create or break alliances.

Seidr's methodology adds another layer to its mystique. I already discussed trance states, but let's not overlook its primary instrument--the 'Seidr staff'--an instrument as crucial to Volva as Thor's hammer is. These staffs weren't simply ordinary sticks either: each Seidr staff featured intricate rune carvings and was sometimes instilled with natural elements for further strengthening its power; acting both as conduit and amplifier for its practitioner's powers--like the Swiss Army knives of magical world magic they proved indispensable and dangerously effective when used properly by skilled practitioners.

Seidr was not solely used for manipulation; it also played an essential role in healing and medicine for ancient Norse folk. Without access to modern pharmacies for aspirin relief, they relied on herbs, rituals, and yes - Seidr - as a form of treatment to address ailments ranging from mundane to supernatural. But its use as medicine tread a fine line between beneficial and detrimental power: techniques which could cure an illness could just as easily bring on new ones; its presence was neither entirely benevolent nor malevolent but profoundly ambivalent.

But the ethics of Seidr are difficult to navigate in an environment which prized honor and valor, yet manipulating fate is something many cultures practiced. Some argue that its moral ambiguity was ideal for exploring Norse ethics - forcing individuals and communities alike to confront what was acceptable versus not acceptable, thus challenging societal norms at once.

At the core of it all lies poetry: Skalds were revered poets from Norse society who used forms of Seidr to write their verses, tapping into its power to stir emotions, inspire warriors and immortalize heroes and events. This poetic aspect added another layer to Seidr: it wasn't just practical but artistic as well, providing a means for self-expression and creativity.

There's a term in Norse mythology called "Wyrd," often understood to represent fate or personal destiny. Seidr was one way of exploring one's Wyrd; in essence, it allowed one to sculpt one's destiny consciously. Unfortunately, Seidr could also create existential anguish: If there was an option available to alter one's fate voluntarily or otherwise - should one take such steps at all? These were important issues any practitioner of Seidr had to confront head on.

At this stage in our exploration of Seidr, it's essential to keep in mind that this practice wasn't simply an afterthought in Norse culture: It played an integral part in it that encompassed both mysticism and reality, the lofty and earthbound; sacred and profane elements alike. Seidr shows us that Norse were more than warriors or sailors - they were thinkers, questioners, and eternal seekers of mysteries both inner and outer. Although gods and heroes often take center stage when discussing Norse mythology stories, let's not forget Volvas and Seidr practitioners as unsung architects of reality who helped weave cosmologies!

2.3.3 Rituals and Ceremonies: Birth, Death, and Marriage

Rituals are the lifeblood of any society, so prepare to enter some of the most intimate and communal aspects of Norse life: birth, death and marriage ceremonies. But don't expect cookie-cutter ceremonies - instead get ready for an adventure filled with symbolism, tradition and--of course!--a bit of divine intervention we all appreciate so much.

Let's begin with birth rituals. Delivering a baby in the Viking Age wasn't just about popping open some champagne and handing out cigars; rather it involved an intricate dance between cosmic forces and mundane reality. Imagine this: just prior to giving birth, women--typically the mother, midwives and close female relatives--would gather in a sacred space. By "sacred space", I don't mean an informal shrine with some incense sticks--I mean an environment purified with herbs and consecrated by ritualistic chants intended to call on protective spirits and ancestral guidance for guidance during labor. Additionally, pregnant mothers may wear amulets such as Thor's hammer for strength or Freyja's boar for fertility to protect both mother and baby during labor.

Remember the Norns? Those fate-weaving goddesses? During birth ceremonies they were believed to be present, literally shaping and measuring a baby's fate with symbolic hands of fate weaving themselves throughout it all. Midwives served as earthly extensions of these divine mistresses of fate while even their first bath could contain layers of symbolism such as water left under moonlight or sunlight to absorb celestial energies - an experience which provided profound connections both between family and the greater cosmos for life itself.

So too was death rituals, the more solemn counterpart to birth ceremonies. One might expect that warrior-oriented societies such as Norse did not view death with fear - for them it was seen more as a transition rather than the end. At this point, the concept of afterlife comes into play. While we all recognize Valhalla, Odin's hall where brave warriors gather and feast eternally, that's only part of it; Hel and Folkvangr also exist where different souls resided. Preparations for life after death were extensive. Deceased would don their finest apparel and carry weapons such as swords, shields and even food and drink with them on their journey into eternity. Their belongings weren't just decorative; they provided essential utility.

Ship burials were an important tradition among chieftains and those with high social standing, representing their vessel carrying their soul across the cosmic sea to their final resting place. But rather than simply sailing off into the sunset, these ships were set ablaze: fire was considered a purifying force that helped free souls of earthly bonds before death occurred. Prior to lighting their funeral pyre, rites would be performed, vows taken, oaths taken and blessings invoked - with many participating as this cosmic event had resonance across dimensions.

Marriage was another stage in life's cycle, or as Vikings would say "joining of threads." Just like birth and death rituals had their own ceremonies, so too did marriage have its own set of rituals - with more pomp. Key elements of Indian wedding ceremonies were the exchange of swords between bride and groom - not as an act to symbolically fight together against life's challenges but instead symbolizing merging two lineages and their protective spirits together; couples also drank "Mead of Poetry", an ancient drink believed to grant them with wisdom and eloquence.

At their core, rituals were like chapters in life's grand narrative arc - orchestrated by divine forces but written and presented by individuals and communities alike. From welcoming a newborn life or paying respects to those who had passed on, to marking union between two hearts or mourning the departure of an individual soul - these rites served as gateways between materiality and spirituality; individualism and collectivism, mortal and divine realms - offering insight into Norse culture's fears, hopes and understanding of reality - like peeling an onion reveals another facet or secret tale.

2.3.4 Viking Ships and Sea Exploration: A Spiritual Voyage

Today we're taking an adventurous voyage aboard Viking ships and sea exploration, but don't think of this as some 'Pirates of the Caribbean' spinoff. Instead, this oceanic venture has much more to do with spirituality than navigation - so grab your compass and metaphysical curiosity; let's embark on our spiritual voyage!

Let's cover the fundamentals: Viking ships were engineering marvels of their time: lightweight, flexible, and fast. Crafted mostly of oak, these vessels could navigate both open seas and narrow rivers easily - with longships being particularly iconic: sleek vessels adorned with intricately carved dragon's head prows to inspire both fear and respect from passersby. However, this wasn't just used as decoration - far from it! The dragon-headed prow was more often than not an effective symbolism used to inspire fear in its passengers! Rather, its presence signaled incoming pirate ships: this creature could sense any approaching threats quickly enough that it would escape in real time from being put together quickly enough.

The dragon or serpent figurehead was more than an aesthetic decoration; it was considered sacred, an amulet designed to protect both ship and crew from harm. Think of it as your spirit animal - Jormungandr or Fafnir was frequently depicted - connecting your journey with cosmic Norse myths through journey talismans such as this complex symbol which represented protection, authority and audacity all at once!

Don't even get me started on sails! These woolen fabric masterpieces were often dyed vibrant hues like reds and blues--often including an accent of symbolic gold--to create an arena of both art and belief. Woven into each thread were intricate patterns or runes meant to invoke divine favor while channeling wind power for salvation. In essence, these sailing temples acted like moving temples as sacred spaces that traversed physical distance between lands while simultaneously traversing metaphysical dimensions.

Of course, ships were only part of the story; crewmembers played an equally critical role. Setting sail on a Viking ship wasn't like taking an overnight flight; rather it was an experience to cherish forever. Each sailor was chosen not only for their physical abilities and navigational prowess, but also to ensure spiritual compatibility with the voyage. Together they formed an unofficial congregation with their own distinct roles within this seafaring ritual. The navigator was often an expert in rune lore and celestial patterns, serving as both priest and spiritual guardian on board ship; the helmsman served as spiritual protector; while rowers provided both muscle power as well as choir harmony to harmonize rhythm of journeys. Even simple sea shanties sung by rowers had layers of spiritual significance hidden within them that went far beyond timekeeping purposes - these songs served as oral traditions that transmitted age-old wisdom tales, invocations and prayers all at once!

Now we come to the most captivating part--the voyage itself. Every Viking expedition was an opportunity for expansion - both materially and spiritually. Imagine it; every voyage into uncharted waters represented an aspect of Norse cosmology whereby the sea symbolized both chaos and opportunity, like venturing into Yggdrasil where each wave represented an adversary and each new land represented another frontier worth discovering.

Each voyage had a purpose that extended beyond physical reality, an endeavor which paralleled spiritual concerns. Not just cartography or exploration; rather it was about charting new spiritual landscapes - with a ship acting as an embodiment of this ideal.

See, the concept of voyage itself was deeply interwoven with Norse cosmology. The crew's task wasn't simply navigating turbulent waters of material reality but also to navigate metaphysical layers of existence - they were part of an immense cosmic narrative with gods, giants, and magical beings from various realms taking part. Imagine playing out an intense live action role-play game involving gods from various realms! Essentially this journey wasn't just geographical; rather it traversed an axis mundi--cosmic axis!

As an exercise in philosophical reflection, consider the sea to be the realm of possibilities and its ship the embodiment of human will and destiny. Both are constantly in dialogue - their meeting point represents chaos and control much like that between Muspelheim and Niflheim in Norse cosmogony. As your ship sails through stormy waters a meditation on life's fleeting but eternal nature unfolds before your eyes - a heavy subject indeed but make no mistake, the journey itself is your goal here!

Once we've navigated through waves and mysticism, the landing is critical. When the ship touched new land it represented a symbolic act of cosmogony--the creation of a new world. Stepping onto unfamiliar soil was heavily ritualistic with offerings to gods and spirits of the land being offered as offerings to celebrate cosmogony in action. Though this may appear mundane at first, its true spiritual impact was immense: this act brought together materiality with divinity by merging human and divine forces into one act that united humans with divine forces while uniting human materiality with divine elements.

Turning back to ships for a moment: after every voyage was complete, ships often found new life as burial vessels for notable individuals who had passed on, carrying their souls closer to Valhalla or Hel. Imagine this! A ship which once traversed mortal seas now serves as a vessel carrying them closer towards Valhalla or Hel - it's poetic justice at sea: turning its voyages from life to death through material to ethereal spaces.

But wait - there's more! These ships, especially longships, were like Swiss Army knives of maritime technology. Beyond their use as warships, trade vessels, and spiritual chariots for Norse people during war and trade missions; longships also became deeply embedded in their culture - becoming symbols of identity representing courage, exploration, spiritual questing ethos of Viking ethos as well as romanticized in sagas and folklore; it was like embedding your soul into wood and sail that became living, breathing entity!

Viking ships and sea exploration were an intricate tapestry of engineering ingenuity, spiritual belief, and cosmic symbolism woven together like an orchestra with each element - material or abstract - playing its part and not forgetting sailors themselves who not only served on Viking ships but were spiritual seekers with souls in harmony with wood, wind and waves.

Book 3: Celtic Mythology

3.1 Exploring the Celtic Otherworld: Gods and Spirits

The Celtic Otherworld is an intricate realm reminiscent of its complex knotwork; here lies gods, spirits, and other mythical entities who inhabit its realms. Far from being some sort of fantastical alternative reality, for Celts it was embedded deeply within nature itself - be it misty hills, dark forests or sacred springs where it thrived beneath. Let's get our boots dirty and set out exploring this fascinating parallel universe together!

Let's begin with an introduction to Celtic gods and spirits. In contrast to some mythologies' deities who reside high up on mountains or heaven, Celtic deities tend to be much closer to Earth - rivers, trees, mountains and more! Brigid is one example: she can be found associated with springs and holy wells as well as springs associated with fertility or poetic arts; when you whisper your prayer or intentions into one dedicated to her it seems almost as if the water ripples in response.

Tuatha De Danann are gods who represent much of what happens in the Otherworld. Originating as deified ancestors of Celts, their involvement spanned war, crafts and love - as well as everything in between!

Famous examples are Lugh, Cu Chulainn and Morrigan (who represent various aspects of war), prophecies and guidance offered by Morrigan - not quite clear-cut good or evil choices but embody human experience to some degree!

As we venture deeper into the Otherworld, you will realize that not just gods and spirits reside there. There's also an assortment of lesser beings such as fairies, banshees and changelings who make an appearance here. Let me set you straight: Celtic fairies differ significantly from their Disney counterparts in that they can bring good fortune or lead people astray depending on their whims - there are even fallen angels known as Gentry who often interact with mortal realms.

But first, we must step back. Any exploration of the Otherworld would be remiss without acknowledging its distinctive topographical features. Celts did not envision this realm as floating above us like an island in the sky; rather it lay underground or underwater accessible through mounds, caves, or wells with entrances at mounds, caves, or wells; picture it: an underground landscape glittering with gems while echoing with haunting melodies and bathed in eternal twilight--something that we cannot see in physical reality!

Keep in mind that in Celtic belief systems, actions have lasting repercussions that go far beyond this world and into the next. "Geis," or binding taboo or obligation, provides a fascinating lens through which to examine ethical dynamics in the Otherworld. These "geasa" range from mundane things such as not eating meat from certain animals to dramatic ones like never refusing a challenge; failing to observe a geis can have dire consequences that affect both worlds - just imagine your fate being held together by an invisible but unbreakable string pulled by unseen hands! That's intense.

Fulfilling obligations or solving riddles often yields divine blessings: magical abilities, remarkable courage or even immortality! King Conchobar found great wisdom from adhering to his geasa contract - another way in which the Otherworld serves as a stage where human decision-making plays out on a cosmic stage; often with gods and spirits acting both as spectators and participants in these interactions.

What I find equally captivating about Celtic mythology is their concept of fate or destiny. While in some mythologies fate is predestined and immutable, in theirs it's much more fluid; here, fate can be altered through actions and choices taken throughout life. Even when fate does make decisions on your behalf, choices still remain open allowing you to steer the direction of your epic narrative with agency remaining intact - making us question its true definition!

But we should never overlook the role of druids and shamans, the original mediators between earthly realms and Otherworld. These individuals were more than simply religious leaders; they served as judges, lore-keepers, gatekeepers of sacred knowledge, unlocked gates to the Otherworld with rituals, and prophecies were highly esteemed as they seemed to come directly from God himself! Their ceremonies carried weight for they drew strength from primal forces that shape both mortal realms as well as Otherworld.

However, for all its magic and allure, the Otherworld should not be seen as some sort of spiritual escape pod from earthly reality. Instead, it serves as a reflection of Celtic worldview with its interplay of free will, destiny, and moral consequence. So as we journey onward, keep this in mind as you travel: This realm isn't simply composed of distant landscapes or otherworldly beings; rather it's us ourselves: Our choices and how we navigate life's maze-like corridors.

3.1.1 Meet the Tuatha Dé Danann: Celtic Gods

Ah, can't you almost hear the wind whispering through those ancient oaks? Welcome to the magic of Celtic realm we are entering now--where gods and goddesses dance not high in the clouds but alongside us; their footsteps hidden by mist or shadow. One family of deities especially representative of this relationship between divine and terrestrial is Tuatha De Danann: hold onto your fascinators and flat caps because this family boasts drama, intrigue and powers worthy of a superhero!

Who are the Tuatha De Danann? Fantastic question! These gods hailing from beyond the North came to Ireland to reclaim what they considered their ancestral land - much like immigrants of old did, but instead wielded spells and mythical weapons instead of visas and paperwork. You may already recognize names like Lugh, Brigid and Dagda; I promise these are just scratching the surface!

Let's begin with Dagda, also known as "Good God," who earned this moniker not so much for moral qualities but due to his exceptional abilities in almost everything - warrior, druid, harpist... He epitomizes all of Tuatha De's multifarious talents: warrior, druid, and harpist rolled into one personified as Dagda; with an ever-fulfilling cauldron and club that can both kill and revive him he truly represents all its talents perfectly; like an all-purpose friend with incredible talent but who remains friendly enough that everyone loves him anyway he/she/she/they all admire/loves them anyway...

Speaking of love, let's move onto Aengus, god of romance, youth, and poetic inspiration who was both conceived and born on the same day! That's incredible medicine! Aengus shows us a different side of Tuatha De: one with romantic ideals and heartfelt pursuits; someone who would top charts with romantic ballads were he still around today - think back to that tale where he dreams of a beautiful maiden and falls head over heels? That's Aengus!

Now let's focus on Brigid, goddess of spring fertility and healing in Celtic mythology. She represents everything from poetry to smithcraft - reflecting her role as part of Tuatha De Danann sabbats such as Imbolc. Bonfires would blaze and offerings placed into wells on Imbolc in tribute to Brigid while praying for lighter days and increased harvests!

But it isn't all roses, my friends! These gods also possess dark sides, complexes and riddles of their own. Take Morrigan - goddess of war, fate and death. She doesn't fit the standard mold of villainy either: instead she could take the form of a crow while simultaneously prophesying doom or helping warriors when necessary. Morrigan represents both life's unpredictability and its transformative power when conflict arises.

And if you think these gods are only about raw power and brute force, think again. Lugh was known as Lugh

Lamhfada or "Lugh of the Long Arm." As such he became known as the God of All Skills because of his proficiency at many arts. From slinging spears with deadly accuracy to plucking harp strings that made heaven weep; Lugh stands as an eternal reminder that divinity can also mean mastery through earthly skills that need perfecting to cosmic might as much as cosmic might.

While we have examined many prominent members of the Tuatha De Danann, what's truly captivating about their organization is the intricate web of relationships, alliances and conflicts among them. If reality TV was around at that time, their tale would certainly make for riveting viewing with its many twists, turns and even sprinkled cosmic magic!

Nuada, the first king of Tuatha De Danann, lost an arm during battle and had to abdicate his throne; most tales would end here; not so with Nuada! Thanks to Dian Cecht (god of healing) and Miach (ancient magical surgeons), Nuada received an artificial silver arm from Dian Cecht (god of healing), with whom Miach assisted as ancient magical surgeons. Thanks to Dian Cecht's influence (or lack thereof!), Nuada got his silver arm back and later reclaimed his throne; thus showing the interconnection among these gods that allowed for balance or chaos depending upon one or another's influence (depending upon which side).

Reminding us to remain in balance is Manannan mac Lir, god of both sea and Otherworld. He serves as an embodiment of journeys across physical seas or metaphysical travels into other realms beyond. Manannan serves as an embodiment of how Celtic mythology depicts worlds with fluid boundaries - his "cloak of mists" may obscure the path leading to divine realms allowing only worthy individuals or even just curious individuals a glimpse of what lies beyond.

Let us also remember Goibniu, the divine blacksmith. Ever wondered where gods got their magical weapons? Goibniu was behind it all - forging blades that never missed and cauldrons that never ran dry - being an embodiment of creativity and craftsmanship that nods towards the importance of artisans in Celtic society. Furthermore, he had an ability to craft an ale that granted immortality - move over craft beers!

Diving deeper into the pantheon, we find figures like Flidais: she serves as an archetype of nature's raw elements while connecting human civilization to nature itself. With Flidais at our side, woodland creatures become sacred beings worthy of honor and reverence.

This exploration of Tuatha De Danann goes far beyond merely telling an intriguing tale about gods and goddesses; it provides an examination of a worldview which views divinity not as remote and distant, but as part of our lives and landscapes - its stories both inspiring and relatable serving as poignant reminders that once existed when human and divine elements overlapped more seamlessly than they do now.

3.1.2 Sidhe and Spirits: The Invisible Dwellers

Like Wi-Fi signals in the air, just because you don't see them doesn't mean they don't exist! In Irish and Scottish traditions, Sidhe are believed to be remnants of Tuatha De Danann who took refuge in sidhe mounds after losing to Milesians (ancestors of modern humans in mythic narrative). It should also be remembered that these hills offer gateways into other realms with fantastical blends between physicality and spirituality that makes these hills unique among their peers.

What sets Sidhe apart is their deep connection to the land. They're not your usual indifferent spirits - these ones have strong opinions about how land should be treated and offending them may result in mysterious illnesses, bad luck or an endless loop of Baby Shark playing in your mind! Conversely, show respect and they might help find that missing sock or ensure that plants grow vibrant and healthy!

Sidhe aren't one-dimensional; their diversity stretches as wide as your musical tastes. Take Banshee for instance; this Irish term refers to her as an embodiment of Bean Sidhe. Far from being the scary monster often portrayed in mainstream media, she serves more as a messenger and prognosticator of doom; when she wails it is not just horror movie scream but anguished song mourning loss of human life; Banshee understands death's gravity while giving us time to prepare ourselves accordingly.

Consider also the Leanan Sidhe, the mysterious spirit world figure who inspires artists while draining their life force, like some sort of fatal attraction. She personifies both the allure and dangers associated with creative passion; like an intense and captivating love affair. Her name stands as an embodiment of both aspects - allure being one and danger the other! This character represents both sides of artistic success: genius or madness and forcing us to question if pursuit of artistic greatness is worth its cost.

The pookas, brownies and kelpies each play their own distinct roles and exhibit distinctive personalities. From shape-shifters playing pranks on humans to household spirits offering assistance directly, their presence fills our world with mystery and wonder.

As it relates to sidhe and other spirits, they encourage us to look beneath the surface and challenge what we think we know about reality. They remind us that reality can be far more fluid and multilayered than we often give it credit for; engaging with them doesn't simply entertain fancy tales but is part of an ethos which recognizes humans' interdependence with nature as seen through unseen sources - a reminder to take a more humble perspective regarding existence; not as the center but as one part among many threads weaving fabric of existence.

Outshone by their mysterious counterparts, there are other spirits worth noting. Take Gruagach for instance; she's like the hipster of the spirit world! Traditionally associated with cattle herding, this curious entity would receive offerings of milk but only the first milk-- this may have been seen as offering first edition vinyl albums of bovine milk! In return she would provide blessings for their herd - truly an indestructible relationship between beast and spirit!

Questions surrounding these spirits center around their meaning and representations of various aspects of life and nature. Taking it further, Aos Si (Celtic Mythology's collective term for spirits and fairies) offers us a lens through which to view and appreciate our world; for the ancient Celts it was believed that every stream, grove and rock had their own spiritual power awaiting discovery - something like Easter eggs of spirituality just waiting to be unearthed!

Don't misunderstand; spiritual reverence isn't simply for charming folktales - it's also a worldview, an approach to our environment that the Celts held dear.

Their worldview believed in an interconnected cosmos in which actions had consequences - this includes actions we take every day that affect spirits that exist as characters within an ongoing narrative involving us all - disrespect them and they could punish you accordingly; honor them and their benefits could multiply immensely.

Consider too that these spirits exist not just across space and time but across generations as well. Their stories have been passed from storyteller to storyteller over generations with each storyteller contributing their own flavor - much like how family recipes tend to change while remaining the same at their core flavors. From oral traditions, medieval manuscripts, and now digital form these stories endure and adapt through time and place.

What can we take away from exploring the realm of Sidhe and other Celtic spirits? For starters, a sense of humility. These stories serve as timely reminders that we share this world with entities beyond our comprehension whose relationships extend far beyond any social network. Secondly, an appreciation for mystery, the sublime and magical qualities which enrich lives beyond all logic or science could ever measure.

These stories offer a mix of life lessons, interwoven with morality, ecology, and even psychology. And while we may never fully grasp its complexity or ethereality, that's okay: exploring it ourselves can be just as rewarding than arriving at any definitive answers.

3.1.3 Landscapes of Power: Sacred Wells and Trees

Let's begin our discussion of sacred wells with these unique locations. A well is much more than simply a hole in the ground where water collects; in Celtic worldview it represents liminal spaces or threshold places between worlds - for instance Connla's Well in Ireland is famously associated with its salmon eating hazelnuts of wisdom - making these waters truly sacred places which were thought to possess healing properties; something akin to ancient health spas!

But here's where it gets really fascinating: people would drop offerings into these wells: coins, pins and cloth of all types were placed as tribute to spirits or made as pleas for favor from them. It wasn't simply throwing money in fountains at malls - this was an exchange of respect or petition to get favor from spirits; an exchange that took place between physical reality and spiritual realms that is rarely experienced today. It is commerce in its purest sense!

Imagine walking through an old-growth forest filled with the smell of damp earth and decaying leaves and coming across an ancient oak that towers majestically above you - it would make an apt visual for Celtic mythology, since this Bile is revered as a symbolic representation between earthly reality and celestial heaven, often found at the center of tribal territories and believed to possess qualities that connected heaven, earth and underworld - almost like spiritual highway traffic rushing up and down its trunk!

Like wells, offerings were made to these trees; however, the stakes were much higher - major ceremonies saw chieftains inaugurated and laws declared on them. Some believed these trees held spirits of ancestors or gods who should not be offended, so harming one was seen as incurring a curse; there even exists the mythological Tree of Life linking all forms of creation similar to its counterpart in Norse mythology Yggdrasil.

Wells and trees in Celtic landscapes weren't simply geographical features: they were part of their belief system that saw divine forces integrated into all aspects of nature, not as distant deities but instead in every living organism. Archaeologists have discovered such locations filled with offerings as proof that these beliefs weren't mere stories; for some Celts still today they serve as means of connecting the visible world to what's unseen - an integral component to life itself.

Imagine this: a sacred well brimming with spiritual significance. While we've already established that these wells were considered places of healing, did you also know they served as settings for divination and omens? Certain wells were said to possess prophetic powers - taking water from them on specific days or during specific planetary alignments was believed to provide insight into future or divine will. Furthermore, elaborate ceremonies would often take place during Celtic festivals like Beltane or Samhain where druids and priestesses would chant incantations while reading patterns in water, leaves or smoke from burnt offerings.

Shifting gears a bit, consider the towering sacred trees. Oak trees weren't the only revered green giants; yew trees also played an integral part in worship rituals. Longevity was another drawcard; many associated longevity with eternal rebirth. Some are even believed to be thousands of years old and given them almost immortal status, echoing eternal life themes found in Celtic myths. Consider: these trees have witnessed both history - when druids performed ceremonies under them to present day churchyards where they stand alone.

Let us not forget, these sacred landscapes were also extremely political. Located at the core of tribal territories, sacred landscapes often became markers of power for chiefs or kings who held control of them - ruling these holy spaces could mean both terrestrial and spiritual influence - so rulers were often inaugurated or crowned in ceremonies conducted here as part of an exercise in both political and spiritual hegemony.

So the scope is vast here. We're speaking of spaces that were both temples and town squares, where spiritual life and daily existence coexisted freely without ever seeming separate or foreign to daily existence. They were an integral part of life that rendered simplistic divides between sacred and secular seem utterly pointless; indeed these magical places still hold some measure of reverence today, although perhaps more as cultural landmarks than spiritual epicenters.

Celtic landscapes like wells and trees served as multilayered symbols, grounded both in cosmic order and earthly reality. Each rock, leaf, pool or river was an unwritten Scripture revealing an endless story with every rainfall or snowfall; from ceremonies, legends or politics they made the Celts who they were.

3.2 Legendary Warriors and Mythical Creatures of Celtic Lore

Celtic mythology boasts an abundance of fantastical beings and legendary heroes woven into its tapestry in ways unique to itself; each contributing their own special brand of magic that continues to capture our collective imagination even today. Don't expect only sword-swallowing fantasy; instead you'll gain insight into values, fears, aspirations of people long past who still captivate our imaginations today - what you get out of reading Celtic mythology is an intimate look into values, fears, inspirational feelings of people living long ago who still resonates within our modern imaginations today that continue captivate us today but continue capturing our imaginations today by living historians writings who wrote it down with vivid detail their values fears aspirations while providing insight into people's values fears aspirations whilst fantasy-think about where Celtic mythology comes from if not then what follows is sure enough!

Imagine fire-breathing dragons with scales harder than any armor, or magical selkies who could transform from seals into beautiful humans, plus legendary warriors like Cu Chulainn who battled so powerfully that even gods had to notice. Indulge yourself with this fantastic adventure! You are surely in for an exciting ride!

This combination of myth and martial arts isn't simply for show; characters and creatures in these tales serve as symbols for deeper cultural truths. Their heroic attributes--be they unwavering courage, unrivaled skill, or tragic flaws--reflect values held dear by Celts; similarly for creatures; they don't just add scare factor; each plays its part in larger moral or cosmological schemes of things.

As we dive deeper into Celtic myth, remember that every character and creature, no matter how outlandish, serves a greater puzzle that weaves its way across Celtic mythology. And it is an astounding puzzle! Are you intrigued? Well, you should be; this journey promises thrilling quests, magical weapons, moral dilemmas that challenge what you know as right and wrong, as well as moral quandaries to put our understanding of right and wrong to the test! Buckle up for an exciting ride - come join us!

3.2.1 Heroes like Cú Chulainn and Fionn mac Cumhaill

Let's begin our exploration of Celtic mythology with two iconic figures, Cu Chulainn (Hound of Ulster). He stands as an antihero figure similar to Hercules; yet with some fascinating characteristics that set him apart. Born as Setanta but later adopting his more familiar title (which literally translates as the Hound of Culann) after accidentally killing a vicious guard dog belonging to Culann, Setanta felt responsible and offered his replacement until another could be trained; now THAT is taking responsibility!

Cu Chulainn was not limited to pet sitting; his prowess as a warrior extended far beyond that. Trained by Scathach and excelling at feats that would make an

Olympic athlete look weak; spear-throwing so precise it could pierce an apple from miles away; swordsmanship that defied physical laws - it seemed as though this man had cheat codes for real life! In Tain Bo Cuailnge (Cattle Raid of Cooley), where he took on entire armies single-handedly before emerging victorious. Yup - this guy really was the real deal!

Fionn mac Cumhaill stands in stark contrast to Cu Chulainn in terms of heroic action; instead he's more like the embodiment of wisdom-seeking warrior, leading the legendary band of fighters known as Fianna. Fionn's tale is similarly impressive but with added mysticism and intellect: born as Demne and transformed by eating Salmon of Knowledge to become Fionn; think Gandalf combined with Napoleon and Sherlock Holmes! And you get some idea why Fionn is such an intriguing figure!

Fionn's exploits were not solely physical; they also explored poetic and philosophical topics. He found equal ease pondering cosmic mysteries as leading his troops into battle - making him a well-rounded hero capable of both muscular and intellectual exertions, embodying Celtic values by representing balanced character traits in one figure.

Now here's the kicker: the stories of Cu Chulainn and Fionn mac Cumhaill aren't just thrilling tales of supernatural feats and epic battles; they also serve as allegories about duty, bravery, wisdom and the complexity of human emotion. While these heroes appear larger-than-life in nature, their human qualities were still evident: from Cu Chulainn's uncontrollable battle frenzy to Fionn's quest for knowledge- these characters had layers upon layers upon layers which have been pulled back and unveiled through generations - creating allegories filled with lessons about duty bravery bravery wisdom wisdom and emotions aplenty that still resonate today.

Fionn was known for his avid pursuit of wisdom, often to an obsessive degree. While being granted immense knowledge from Salmon of Knowledge was immense, its weighty responsibility came at the cost of alienating others who didn't understand his depth of thoughts or burden of knowledge - an unfortunate price to pay! Yet Fionn still managed to maintain an attractive leadership quality which gained him loyalty among the Fianna warriors under him.

Fionn was also a cultural hero. Aside from his military exploits, Fionn is associated with creating Ireland's geographical features; according to legend, he even cast a piece of Ireland into the sea which later formed into the Isle of Man! While Cu Chulainn left his mark through battle-based accomplishments alone, Fionn made his legacy endure through stories, landscapes and wisdom that still survive today.

One cannot help but be struck by the contrast between these two heroes. Cu Chulainn often serves as an embodiment of youthful exuberance, diving headlong into battle guided by moral principles but still being led by emotions like passion or anger. By contrast, Fionn is the more seasoned warrior, someone whose experience has taught him to carefully consider his options before acting upon them - Cu Chulainn could be compared to a raging fire while Fionn could represent its glowing ember - both have energy but at different stages in life, manifested differently!

Before we conclude this discussion, let's briefly consider the legacy of these heroes. Their tales have not merely remained within mythology's pages - rather, they have permeated into folklore of all kinds - impacting literature, art and political debate alike. Their iconic status has allowed various causes and ideologies to use them as symbols of ideal traits such as Cu Chulainn and Fionn mac Cumhaill as evergreen reminders of ideal qualities that they represent. These figures have become part of Celtic collective consciousness; these iconic figures represent archetypes deeply embedded within its collective consciousness - both exist as archetypes deep within its collective consciousness of Celtic world culture!

So what's the takeaway here? These heroes embody the virtues that were valued by Celtic people: bravery, wisdom, love and their complex interrelation. Not just cool stories but glimpses into ancient cultures' souls as their multidimensional characters reveal different aspects of human nature while appreciating how strength coexisted with wisdom, duty and duty, humanity and divinity in an interdependent manner.

3.2.2 Creatures from Banshees to the Morrigan

Let's begin with Banshees; their mere mention might give you chills! Originating in Irish folklore as "bean sidhe," meaning "woman of the fairy mound," these mysterious beings have long been considered portents of death and other grim fates. Before jumping to Hollywood's portrayal of banshees as evil beings, take note: They can often be more nuanced. In many stories, banshees do not cause death themselves but mourn its arrival with haunting wails heard when someone near death is about to die. She is closely associated with Irish families and acts as an ancestral matriarch figure. Although sometimes seen as frightening, her lament shouldn't necessarily be taken as something to fear but could instead be seen as an expression of love, marking an ending or helping to guide one into the afterlife. Like an unofficial town crier who only ever shows up at really big life events!

Interesting too is how the banshee appears in various forms; sometimes she's an attractive young woman, at other times an old hag, or sometimes an animal associated with witchcraft, like a crow or hare. Her shape-shifting makes her not just a symbol of death but transformation; you are witnessing a tradition exploring life through its multidimensional aspects - isn't that impressive?

Irish mythology's Morrigan (or Phantom Queen) is an intricate web. She represents war, fate, death, sexuality and fertility - not to mention being depicted as three sisters named Badb, Macha and Nemain. Each represents different aspects of life and death while simultaneously acting as warrior queen or prophetess for various roles ranging from battle field mortality crows or even seducing Cu Chulainn herself!

Attracted to Morrigan by her complex nature is its irreducibility - neither completely good or evil; instead she defies easy categorizations. For instance, in one tale she foretold death for Cu Chulainn; yet in another she offered his wounds relief with milk from her cow! That makes the Morrigan both storm and shelter! Her contradictions reflect life itself; Celtic mythology takes no pains to obscure this.

See, depictions of these creatures don't just serve storytelling purposes; their multidimensional personalities reflect ancient Celtic societies' views on women's roles and gender fluidity. Women in Celtic societies held significantly higher status compared to many other ancient civilizations - they could serve as warriors, rulers and druids--roles which went far beyond expectations at that time. By looking at characters like Morrigan as both warrior and healer or banshee as both compassionate mourner and fearsome apparition, one is basically seeing into ancient societies' cultural ideals!

And this mythological creature does more than just reflect human introspection; they also serve to illustrate the Celtic peoples' intricate relationship with nature. Morrigan's connection to crows and banshee's connection to certain landscapes such as rivers or mounds underscore this notion - as though each creature, hill, stream and river had its own tale to share; indeed the Celts lived in an intense world where meaning abounded between natural and supernatural elements and was often deliciously blurry.

Have you ever considered why myths endure for so many centuries? One answer lies within adaptability - these tales change over time to include elements from various cultures and religious practices; for instance, banshee legends have made their way into American folklore among communities with Irish ancestry, while Morrigan imagery can now be found everywhere from T-shirts to modern literature; proof that ancient legends remain relevant today!

Let's now examine their impact. While banshees and the Morrigan may make for captivating campfire stories, their myths carry profound emotional and psychological weight. Banshee wails can serve as an emotional release valve, providing voice for community grieving or sorrow; Morrigan provides insight into experiences such as war, love, or personal growth - these tales don't just serve as entertainment; rather they reflect a reality embedded deep within human experience, yet hidden under layers of myth but nonetheless resonate timeless truth.

3.3.3 The Importance of Animals in Celtic Myths

Celtic mythology features many fascinating animals as key players who hold significant meaning for its narratives; from the hounds of Cú Chulainn to salmon of wisdom, animals play more than simply symbolic roles; they provide an in-depth examination of what defines a Celtic worldview.

Take, for instance, salmon: Celtic mythology holds it up as being among the oldest and wisest creatures on Earth. Ever heard of Ireland's Salmon of Knowledge? According to legend, it swam in Well of Segais eating hazelnuts fallen from nine nearby hazel trees before finally being devoured by those lucky enough to consume this fish as nourishment for wisdom gaining. Now consider why that was appropriate: salmons are known for making long journeys upstream which were seen by Celts as symbols of wisdom seeking and all its trials along the way in pursuit of wisdom attainment.

Let us not forget birds such as the raven or crane, popular symbols in Celtic art and tales. In many myths, these birds represent more than battlefield emblems; they also signify transformation and cosmic order. Ravens were considered messengers between this world and the Otherworld - crossing over life-and-death boundaries and beyond - much like our previous discussion on Morrigan, who often transformed herself into ravens! These transformative elements demonstrate how animals serve as an important link between different planes of existence - essential pieces for understanding Celtic perspectives on life, death and what lies beyond.

But we simply can't leave out land mammals! Consider the stag, associated with Cernunnos in Celtic mythology, and white boar, which often leads heroes on quests in Welsh legend. Both animals were deeply tied to the land and forests revered by Celts; their appearance in these tales not random but reflective of their harmony with their environment - these animals even served as guides and protectors of it; embodying qualities like courage, wisdom, and virility for ancient Celts.

Domestic animals like cattle had their place in mythological storytelling as well. Cows, for instance, were considered extremely valuable by Celts not only due to their economic worth but also for the symbolic meanings associated with fertility and abundance they held symbolic of. In Tain Bo Cuailnge (The Cattle Raid of Cooley), war between Connacht and Ulster is waged over an extremely valuable brown bull in an epic that explores intricate social, political, and cosmic dynamics at play in its tale.

The Celts had an extensive tradition of shapeshifting. People would change shape into animals or vice versa. What does that tell us? It represents identity fluidity and interconnectivity of life forms. So the transformation isn't literal but allegorical as well: when someone turns into a bird or when goddesses assume bear forms they encourage us to consider the transient nature of existence and grapple with questions like who we are as individuals, or indeed, as creatures in this vast universe?

Let's take a detour and discuss magical beasts for a bit, shall we? Examples include creatures such as the Griffin - part eagle, part lion, yet completely majestic; or the Kelpie, an aquatic spirit with shape-shifting abilities who takes the form of a horse? These mythical beings don't simply exist as abstract concepts: they represent complex amalgamations of animal traits representing Celts' nuanced understanding of nature's dualities: good and evil, beautiful yet terrifying - carrying lessons about accepting these paradoxical forces that shape life itself.

Aren't animals great! Have you noticed how integral animals are to a hero's journey? From loyal companions to cunning tricksters, these characters often serve as catalysts in the hero's internal struggles, reflecting this onscreen through moral decisions made in dealing with these creatures like loyal companions or cunning tricksters? Animal characters act as ethical litmus tests by showing us who these heroes truly are, while imparting invaluable moral lessons that transcend filmic genres and into real life situations.

On an unexpected turn of events: let's discuss the ritualistic aspect of these animals. The Celts didn't only include animals in their myths; they incorporated them into daily rites and ceremonies such as animal sacrifices or using animal totems for protection, showing their profound regard for nature. Furthermore, seeing divine power within all living beings elevated the status of animals within spiritual and ethical frameworks.

Once all these threads come together - transformation, magical beasts, ethical dilemmas and ritualistic practices--they create a complex tapestry revealing the heart and soul of Celtic spirituality and morality. Animals in Celtic myths serve more than as mere sidekicks or symbols: They become living characters who reflect deep thoughts about existence, morality and the natural world.

3.3.4 Epic Quests and Adventurous Sagas

If you love storytelling, Celtic myths offer a distinctive way of unfurling their tales; rather than linear storytelling, we encounter cycles of stories which weave in and out of one another leaving tantalizing loose ends which get picked up later - much like an intricate Celtic knot itself! This narrative structure captures how Celts view time cyclically rather than linearly by emphasizing interconnected events, characters, and moral lessons!

Now, let's delve deeper into these quests. Celtic heroes often set out in search of magical artifacts or hidden knowledge, reflecting our human desire for exploration and illumination. One such quest in Welsh Mabinogion involves searching for the Cauldron of Rebirth; not only does this object possess miraculous powers but its pursuit raises intriguing questions about life, death and existence itself - not simply serving as plot device but instead acting as philosophical enigma designed to challenge and tease your intellect!

Are You Up For an Interesting Plot Twist? Oftentimes, quests have unexpected outcomes that defy traditional "happily ever after" endings, with heroes often meeting their goals at great personal cost - often their homeland or loved ones being sacrificed along the way. Such unexpected plot turns are meant as reminders that life is complicated, messy and unpredictable like its very myths which tell these tales.

Do you ever find yourself wondering about the antagonists in these quests? These adversaries don't exactly fit the stereotypical mold of villains - instead they feature complex figures with their own motivations and moral dilemmas that mirror those faced by our hero, as he or she navigates a maze of choices and consequences with equally dire results - adding another level of moral ambiguity that elevates these tales beyond mere storytelling into insightful examinations of human nature and morality that have us considering questions such as: "What makes someone a hero or villain?" And the answers often surprise us!

Not content to stop there, these quests also serve as rites of passage for our heroes, forcing them to confront their deepest fears and weaknesses head-on. Not just physical in nature; the journey is psychological as well. Our heroes emerge from these adventures transformed; having gained wisdom, strength or renewed sense of purpose. At its heart lies this essential theme: these adventures serve as transformative journeys that impart invaluable life lessons not only to ourselves as readers or listeners but also the characters themselves.

Celtic mythology illustrates this beautifully, where magic and reality coexist seamlessly in an interdependent fashion.

At its heart lies an intriguing realization: these magical elements in these stories don't exist solely to amuse. Instead, they often serve as metaphors for deeper psychological or existential truths. Take for instance the "Otherworld," a parallel dimension where heroes encounter death, unconscious forces or existential terrors. While you might not encounter mythical creatures every day on your commute to work, we all face our own "Otherworlds," whether dealing with complex emotions or making difficult life decisions.

Switching gears, let's examine the vital role that mentors play in these quests. They act like guides who guide Obi-Wan Kenobi or Gandalf; Celtic heroes often have wise druids or magical guides who provide wise counsel and moral compass advice; these mentors serve more than practical purposes - they illuminate a path towards virtue and wisdom - prompting one to ask who their own mentors might be - those that help shape our moral fiber while encouraging us when times get tough?

Have you noticed how music, poetry and song play an integral role in these adventures? They don't simply serve for entertainment or mood setting--in Celtic stories music often has transformative powers; healing, enlightening and even altering reality! Think back on how art and music have affected your own life--perhaps they have had similar transformative powers?

One interesting tidbit for you: adventures often feature trials or tests - often three in number - similar to what the Celts saw as symbolizing completeness and balance. Trials serve as initiation rites where heroes prove themselves not just through courage but moral virtue, wisdom and even humility - life lessons packaged into challenges designed to test limits of adventurers.

At their core, Celtic mythological epic quests are more than thrilling tales filled with action and danger; they're intricate tapestries of symbolism, ethics and philosophical truths woven together like an intricate tapestry. Readers should actively participate by questioning and exploring these tales of old. Perhaps initially thought as mere bygone tales from another time period; now hopefully you realize they hold timeless wisdom relevant to any age and stage in life.

3.3 Druids, Bards, and Keepers of Wisdom

Druids, Bards and Keepers of Wisdom Ahh... the Druids, Bards, and other Keepers of Wisdom mes These figures in Celtic legend represent scholars, artists, spiritual gurus all-in-one. Sadly, however, they're often reduced to mere "wise old men and women who did mystical things". But don't underestimate them: these fascinating individuals played key roles in building thought, culture and even the spiritual universe within Celtic lore and history.

Imagine this: a Druid draped in an emerald green cloak standing under moonlight within an ancient sacred grove; or a Bard, with not just his sword but harp in hand, cutting through the air with songs of valor and heartache. These figures weren't simply "magicians" or "priests," though; rather they provided essential services as keepers of stories, laws, traditions and social bonds which kept Celtic communities together; Druids and Bards provided crucial social ties while giving voice to society at large.

Even without Google, Wikipedia or even a decent library as we know them today, Druids were the closest thing Celtic societies had to search engines in terms of knowledge acquisition. Revered for their knowledge in astronomy, medicine, law, philosophy and religious rites they advised kings on healing the sick while mediating between humanity and gods at times. Religiously they performed rituals but more importantly as teachers, scientists, historians or simply orally passing along important information from one generation to the next.

Do not forget the Bards! Ah, the Bards--poets, musicians, and storytellers extraordinaire. Their job was to capture the essence of an age's heroes, woes, triumphs, tragedies through song. Imagine sitting in a smoky torch-lit hall as one of these Bards regales the crowd with tales of heroic deeds or tragic love; their songs could rally troops to battle, immortalize heroes into folklore stories or even heal or transcend life beyond earthly dimensions - giving newfound respect to playlist power than ever before!

3.3.1 Who Were the Druids and What Was Their Role?

mFirst things first—where does the word "Druid" even come from? If you dig into etymology, you'll find the term has its roots in ancient Celtic words like *dru-wid-s*, which is often translated to mean "oak-knower" or "oak-seer." Kind of poetic, right? In an age where nature was seen as a force to be reckoned with, enigmatic knowledge about one tree represented something more profound: it was associated with strength and wisdom that Druids aimed to embody.

Education-wise, to become a Druid one had to undergo a rigorous learning period that often lasted two decades - no online certificates or weekend seminars here! Druids-in-training were taught orally, matching Celts' high regard for oral language as they covered everything from history, law, astronomy, poetry philosophy and sacred rites - some Druids were even so skilled with memory techniques they could recite epic poems or historical records for days at once! Makes high school history finals seem so easy doesn't it?

What were their day-to-day roles? During peacetime, Druids were often found serving as trusted advisors to kings and leaders, offering counsel on everything from governance and law to astronomy and agriculture. Druids were polymaths of old, experts across multiple fields who enjoyed exemption from military service and taxes; all without incurring everyday stressors that plagued other professions. This unique position granted them time for study, reflection and providing counsel without worrying about everyday pressures plaguing other professions had to endure.

But let's not forget, they also had spiritual duties to fulfill. Druids were responsible for performing various religious rites related to lunar and solar cycles as well as life events like births, marriages and deaths - as written words were thought to lessen their impact all ceremonies were performed from memory by Druids.

Their understanding of celestial movements wasn't simply for show; rather it played an integral part in spiritual practices like harvesting crops early or hunting seasons that often began earlier because celestial signs were provided by Druidic knowledge and celestial signs.

Warfare changed their role dramatically. Though exempt from fighting, Druids were never just spectators on the sidelines. Instead, they often accompanied armies onto battlefields not as combatants but as spiritual advisors and leaders. Picture this: an elderly Druid lifting their staff above his troops while incantations to invoke divine favor or strike fear into enemies were being chanted; even Roman armies, not used to such tactics themselves, were said to have been deeply unnerved by Druid presence among Celtic ranks!

Druids were known to cause shockwaves among Roman armies, so you can imagine they held great influence within their communities as well. Druids played an instrumental role in legal matters too; often being called upon to arbitrate disputes such as property lines disputes and rival clan feuds between rival clans. Their rulings were rarely challenged. Imagine having the power to change individual lives as well as entire communities by means of your wisdom and understanding of ancient customs!

However, not everything was all rosy for these spiritual leaders; Druids also practiced dark arts and mysticism in addition to believing in the Otherworld - an alternative realm where spirits and deities resided. Druids were instrumental in connecting our world to this ethereal realm, using rituals and incantations to reach out and connect with spirits. Divination and augury practices allowed them to predict future events or seek guidance. But here's where it gets weird: these ancient societies also believed in human sacrifice as a means of appeasing their gods and maintaining equilibrium within their world. Although often exaggerated in popular culture, historical evidence points towards its existence - although probably far less frequently than popular media portrays.

Speaking of perception, what do we really know about Druids? One difficulty in grasping them lies with our lack of firsthand accounts from them; most information comes from Roman writers like Julius Caesar and Pliny the Elder who may have their own biases and agendas when depicting Druids as barbaric and savage; these depictions could have been exaggerated to justify Roman conquests, so our view of them as mysterious figures conducting arcane rituals in secretive groves could well be more rooted in legends or propaganda than historical fact.

The Druids have experienced an extraordinary cultural decline. After the Roman invasion and subsequent

Christianization of Britain, Druidism began to decline rapidly as new religious ideologies gained ground - monasteries replaced groves, Latin prayers took their place among ancient, monasteries were built instead, monasteries replaced groves and Latin prayers replaced ancient Celtic chants; yet remnants of Druidic practices remain embedded into folklore and local customs; even today there exists modern versions of Druidry that seeks to revive these ancient traditions while giving modern practitioners permission to interpret ancient traditions while adapting them for 21st-century audiences.

But let's not get too caught up in a "rise and fall" narrative; Druids have left an impressive legacy that far outlives just their historical incarnations. Their presence can still be felt everywhere from popular culture to spiritual practices; their legacy resonates today through popular culture to spiritual practices - popularly as wise sages, keepers of ancient secrets, mediators between worlds or whatever role you ascribe them as. Whether seen as teachers, mystical shamans or something in between; their legacy stands testament to humanity's many facets!

3.3.2 The Power of Oral Tradition: Bards and Storytellers

In Celtic society, which was characterized by Druidic religious and judicial authority at its pinnacle, Bards and storytellers played an essential role in weaving a tapestry of culture and history that united communities. Not just entertainers or minor functionaries; Bards were the living repository of generations worth of lore, customs, identity; through every string plucked on their harp or spoken verse they created a sense of shared consciousness that outlived time and space.

Consider this: the Celts didn't develop written language until they encountered Roman alphabet letters, yet their oral tradition was an intricate system for passing down knowledge. Bards were remembered keepers. Their stories weren't simply entertaining; they served as historical documents, moral lessons and legal decrees all wrapped into poetic verse. Imagine gathering around a fire, the flickering light casting animated shadows on their faces as all eyes focus on an epic tale about its creation and touching on themes such as courage, wisdom and honor. That would be just one scenario!

Now you might be asking how these tales managed to stay consistent through several generations, well the Bardic tradition was extraordinarily disciplined: in order to become a bard, one needed to undergo years of intensive training, memorizing verse, mastering rhyme and meter, and developing an acute understanding of human nature - making stories resonate with each new audience. Not just someone sitting around playing guitar at a campfire - these professionals were true scholars, performers, and keepers of cultural heritage!

Bards weren't simply limited to storytelling; they also served as composers of eulogies and praise-poems for nobility. In a society where reputation was as valuable as wealth, Bards could use their words to either elevate someone's social standing or bring about their downfall; some eulogies could take days or even years to read in full! Imagine having such power: in their words rested the ability to alter public perception for generations--like going viral but with lasting consequences--in fact it could change forever!

Storytelling wasn't simply one-sided; audiences played an essential part. Collective experiences like listening to a tale with gasps, laughs and tears all play an integral part of interactive storytelling at its finest. A Bard would often adjust his stories according to how their audiences responded; if something struck a nerve with audiences he may extend that part further in subsequent retellings for increased emotional response - making oral tradition an ever-evolving art form and guaranteeing you'd hear the same tale at different points throughout life with each experience tailored exactly according to that particular audience's temperaments and experiences!

Let's address one other important aspect of bardic work, specifically their myth-making ability. Alongside historical documents and moral tales, bardic repertoire also included stories that explored supernatural topics. Mythical animals such as gods, spirits and legendary beasts weren't just stories for children to enjoy; they served as allegorical tools to discuss complex topics like morality, destiny and the nature of reality. These myths could be seen as precursors of science, serving to explain how and why the world works before scientific method was ever employed. Just as modern-day physicists use complex equations to reveal time-space relationships, ancient Bards would use tales about deities and heroes to explore its mysteries.

Bards employed various mnemonic devices to aid them in remembering their vast repertoire, from spirals and knots in Celtic art, through knotted key patterns, to spirals. There have been theories suggesting these designs served a dual function as both decorative and memory aids; think about every curve or twist being coded for specific characters, events or moral lessons - that gives you some sense of just how complex their Bardic "database" could have been!

Even the Celtic harp, the Bard's musical companion, served multiple purposes. Not just an instrument, it provided mnemonic reminders, rhythm keepers and emotional intensifiers; its strings could correspond with different tales or characters being told; music also helped engage audiences by accentuating highs and lows of stories being told, making their tales not just heard but felt.

Let us now address the impact of historical change on Bardic tradition, particularly Christianization. Christianity presented Bards with a complex dilemma. On one hand, clergy saw value in Bardic memorization and storytelling practices; some monasteries became training grounds where Christian themes began seeping into traditional narratives. On the other hand, however, religious authorities often saw these tales -- especially ones featuring pagan gods or practices -- as heretical. As Christianity spread further, Bards found themselves walking a fine line between cultural preservation and religious blasphemy as their influence grew stronger.

Rome added another twist to the Bardic tradition with their written language; potentially rendering oral storytelling obsolete but instead providing bards a way to immortalize their stories through written records; even if this meant some lost of their dynamic flair over time.

However, in spite of these challenges and shifts, the Bardic tradition did not simply survive; it flourished. From spoken word performances and written texts, to digital media like novels, films and video games that explore Celtic mythology today. We owe an enormous debt of gratitude to ancient Bards who first shared these tales, as well as to communities who listened, engaged with them, and passed them down from generation to generation.

3.3.3 Sacred Groves and Ritualistic Practices

Let's set the scene, literally speaking. Sacred groves played an essential role in Celtic cosmology, serving as centers where human life and the Otherworld interacted most directly. Imagine: an isolated woodland area hidden from prying eyes where ancient oak trees stand tall like wise elders while damp earth and foliage scent fills the air - this scene may sound poetical enough; but what truly made these groves amazing was their inherent spiritual power.

Trees were symbols of wisdom and energy, with each species embodying specific qualities - oak was the king of trees, representing strength and durability; hazel symbolized wisdom; rowan was associated with protection. Even choosing the location for ritual required deciphering the symbolic meanings of surrounding trees to find one most suited to meeting ritualistic goals.

These groves served as the location for various ceremonies and celebrations, such as Druidic initiation ceremonies or seasonal festivities such as Beltane or Samhain celebrations. Also notable was their role as venues for rituals connected with birth, death, and rebirth which echoed nature's eternal cycles of birth, death, and rebirth. Their atmosphere was electric with participants holding tight to their beliefs as high emotional stakes of ritual rites took place here. Druids would often demarcate these sacred spaces by drawing circles or placing stones within it to increase its intensity even further - further amplifying its energy!

Rituals were breathtaking experiences designed to alter states of consciousness and facilitate communion with the divine, often featuring incantations sung or chanted by Druids and Bards with drum beats punctuating by drum tones and the melodies of harps; Herbal concoctions created under specific astrological conditions could also be consumed, serving both medicinal and psychoactive purposes; divination ceremonies would often include Ogham staves, runes or other oracular tools held and cast by adept seers to forecast future developments or uncover answers for pressing issues.

Given the confidential nature of Celtic rituals, accurate details are understandably scarce. What we know comes mostly from fragments of texts or secondhand accounts written by outsiders--often Romans--with their own biases and misconceptions; nonetheless these glimpses offer us a rich tapestry of practices which offer insights into Celtic worldview.

Holy wells were an integral part of Druidic societies long before Christianity, yet were quickly integrated into Christian landscape. Though often rebranded with images or blessings from Christian saints, their rituals remained strikingly similar: people still turned to them for healing powers for ailments just like they had during Druidic times; offerings were still made, though instead of trinkets or votive gifts to Celtic deities they now bore symbols like crosses or saints' images as offerings.

As with the sacred groves, sacred spaces didn't simply vanish - they were transformed. Some became locations for churches or monasteries to conveniently take advantage of their already magical energies. Both religions recognized a common ground when it comes to sacred space - instead of unraveling this thread altogether, both embroidered it with new designs - even Beltane fires that had once celebrated summer's arrival were adopted into Christian traditions as need-fires believed to protect cattle against disease.

Yet despite these adaptations, aspects of old ways clung on, especially in rural areas away from organized religion's influence. Here one can find remnants of ancient Celtic practices; such as rituals performed under cover of night or talismans kept hidden away within homes as well as secret gatherings in still-existing sacred groves - each iteration adding new layers of meaning and interpretation as generations passed them down through generations like family recipes.

As Druidic oral tradition was eventually translated into written form - often years after its original context had passed - monasteries became the place where these texts could be found, often Christianized manuscripts that still held remnants of ancient wisdom that lie buried deep within their pages like fossilized remnants waiting to be unearthed by someone with keen eyes.

Aren't we surprised? It is truly remarkable how two competing belief systems, instead of colliding head on, found ways to coexist and even enrich each other. Imagine Druidism and early Christianity being two streams that joined to form one river where each stream contributed currents that helped forge stronger spiritual practices and beliefs that enhanced each other.

As you stroll through a tranquil grove or come upon an ancient well, take a moment to reflect. Your very feet have stood witness to centuries of spiritual quests; its soil has stored away secrets whispered under moonlight and hymns sung into dawn light; not just soil and stone but a living archive of human efforts to touch divinity.

3.3.4 The Ogham: An Alphabet Wrapped in Mystery

Before we explore its layers, let's get some basics out of the way: Ogham is an early Medieval alphabet used to represent Old Irish language. The characters, or "letters," consist of a series of notches and diagonal or horizontal lines carved into wooden staves or stone monuments - often used as markers indicating rituals or cultural norms within its surrounding context. However, its mystery does not just lie within physical form alone: you might come across Ogham script inscriptions that make you question its purpose in terms of both physical form and context: there could be deeper meaning attached to these etchings?

Historians and linguists alike have long debated the origins of Ogham with great passion. Theories range from native Celtic invention to external influences like runic alphabets of Germanic tribes or even Latin alphabet, making for fascinating discussion. Unfortunately, no consensus has yet been reached and that's precisely why it remains such an intriguing debate: just when you think you understand something fully, another curveball comes along that sends you backward.

Are you asking, what was the primary purpose of this mysterious script? Excellent question! Ogham writing initially used short inscriptions, and today you may still come across Ogham stones in Ireland, Wales or Scotland - silent reminders of history - dotted around. Ogham stones often bear the names of individuals and places, leading historians to assume they served as territorial markers or memorials. Don't mistake Ogham for just another form of graffiti - in some instances its poetic nature suggests Ogham was also used by learned individuals such as Druids to communicate religious or philosophical messages encrypted using Ogham symbols.

Ogham can also be associated with supernatural elements. Within Celtic belief systems, letters and words possess inherent power--think of it as linguistic alchemy. To add another layer of mysticism, Ogham symbols correspond with specific trees or plants--an important feature given their animistic roots. Could Druids have used Ogham script in their rituals or as talismans? Again, all speculation with an element of maybe.

But wait a second--now is where technology and history meet! Thanks to modern archaeological methods and computational linguistics, deciphering Ogham has become an interdisciplinary pursuit; algorithms join hands with folklore and historical texts as we slowly unravel its secrets line by line - each discovery sheds more light onto this ancient artifact while paradoxically becoming even more complicated!

Ogham is more than an alphabet; it's an intriguing, multilayered puzzle waiting to be explored, combining practical and spiritual elements in its composition and providing us with access to an illuminating heritage that continues to confound and mystify all those who try to decode its secrets.

Recall how we discussed Ogham's connection with nature, specifically trees. Each character not only represents sound but also corresponds with specific trees or plants such as Birch Oak Hazel; each has an Ogham character representing sound that corresponds with them - it's as though Celts designed this script so it communicates directly with nature! Why was this important? In a society which revered nature such as Celtic ones did, embedding these symbols could have imparted special powers or spiritual resonance - imagine carving words onto wooden staves knowing these characters would connect directly with its elemental links! It's like poetry meets ecology had one tiny baby... and its name is Ogham!

Now, let's talk about its structure for a second. The basic Ogham alphabet consists of 20 characters grouped into four sets of five. These are called aicmí (say it like "ack-mee," go on!). But hold your horses, because there are also five additional "forfeda," or special characters, used for sounds that aren't represented in the original 20. Talk about an alphabet that evolves to meet the needs of its users, right?

Are You Curious About How Ogham Was Written and Carved? Let us dispel some misconceptions Now. It was not written left-to-right or top-bottom; rather it was written along its edges - think of a stone or wooden stave as its canvas; start from bottom left, move up then down then back left again for its signature appearance and additional complexity of decipherment.

Ogham's relationship to Celtic mythology and cosmology is particularly captivating: in several Irish legends it appears as an obscure form of knowledge used for divination, prophecy or magical spell casting. Legends ascribe Oghma as having created Ogham as a way of communicating with divine forces or transcending barriers between human life and supernatural entities like spirits or gods.

Ogham's modern revivals and adaptations should not be overlooked either; contemporary Druids and Neo-Pagans alike use Ogham in their rituals and spiritual practices, providing another prime example of how ancient systems can be reinterpreted to take on new meaning in modern contexts - whether that means being sold on Etsy as handmade crafts or used for divination methods in divination methods used today, Ogham successfully bridges both worlds.

Book 4: Egyptian Mythology

4.1 Life Along the Nile: Deities of Egyptian Mythology

Ah, the Nile River! A vital source of life that helped sustain an entire civilization! Ancient Egyptians considered this serpentine waterway a divine entity tied to their myths, beliefs and daily lives. Imagine having the entirety of your existence supported by a river and monitored by deities who represent both nature's forces and aspects of human experience. Each deity holds their own special role in the celestial drama that plays out along the riverbanks, from Horus with his hawk-head to Sekhmet with her lioness goddess status. Buckle up as we're about to dive deep into the mysteries surrounding these divine beings - how they were worshiped, their stories surrounding them, and their profound influence upon one of history's most fascinating civilizations. I assure you, the waters of the Nile run with mythology. So let's set sail and discover more about those deities who guided life along its banks!

4.2.1 An Overview of Gods like Ra, Osiris, and Isis

We could talk for hours about Egyptian gods and goddesses; let's narrow it down to three superstars of divinity--Ra, Osiris and Isis--who dominate ancient Egyptian life as religious figures as well as daily living situations, politics and natural elements.

Beginning with Ra, the sun god, this deity enjoyed one of the strongest followings in ancient Egypt. Worshiped as both patron of pharaohs and patron of their gods, Ra was believed to travel across the sky in two solar boats--one for morning and one for evening sailings--in a daily rhythm symbolic of his voyages. People didn't just admire Ra; their daily lives revolved around it: Egyptian daily routine revolved around sun's journey that symbolized Ra's journey; indeed setting sun meant Ra's descent into chaos underworld where his victory or reappearance was never certain - reinforcing fragility of order and life itself.

Osiris was an intriguing god. Although best-known as the patron of the afterlife, Osiris also held great power over vegetation and was considered an ideal form of kingship. His mythology includes betrayal, death and resurrection - even being mummified himself! Osiris Mysteries offered hope of eternal blissful afterlives for those participating.

Isis, Osiris' sister and wife, is another goddess who needs no introduction. Worshiped as the ideal mother and wife as well as patron of magic and healing, after Osiris was murdered and dismembered by Set's jealousy she used her magic abilities to restore Osiris back to life temporarily - showing great love, devotion, and power - her story being one of immense love devotion power as her cult spread far beyond Egypt to include even Roman empire!

It's fascinating to observe how these gods and goddesses don't exist as standalone characters in an underlying cosmic drama; instead they play important roles that overlap and overlap again with one another. And don't even get me started on their symbology! Whether Ra's solar disk or Osiris's crook and flail have special significance for each deity and can reveal even deeper layers of meaning with their iconography associated with them - like Ra's solar disk for Ra or Osiris crook and flail or Ra's solar disk for Osiris - their symbology speaks volumes in its own unique language rich with symbolism that can uncover deep layers of meanings!

Let's go further into the complexity of Egyptian life; take a peek into tombs or temples; you will likely spot hieroglyphs depicting Ra, Osiris and Isis alongside other gods, mythical creatures and elements carved into tomb walls - an indication of their importance as pieces in maintaining Ma'at, the ancient Egyptian concept of cosmic order and balance.

Imagine Ma'at as the gravitational pull in this galaxy of myths. Each deity contributes to this celestial order in their own ways - Ra's journey does not simply represent light; rather it represents his daily battle against Apep, an embodiment of chaos and disorder who opposes him daily. Meanwhile Osiris' resurrection signified his triumph over mortality while reinforcing Egyptian belief in eternal life through hope renewal and cycles such as flooding of the Nile River that sustained Egypt agriculture.

As for Isis, her appeal transcends mythology and permeates real life. She was revered as the goddess embodiment of qualities ancient Egyptians found endearing: loyalty, cleverness and tenacity. During her role in bringing Osiris back to life she did so not solely out of ritualistic action but due to being herself an extension of these traits - an empowering message especially for women that compassion and ingenuity can be powerful forms of strength.

Egypt's sociopolitical fabric was intricately interwoven with these deities. Pharaohs often invoked Ra to legitimize their rule by emphasizing their divine lineage; temples dedicated to these gods served not just as places of worship; they were centers for learning, healthcare, justice and agricultural cycles - priests with knowledge in Osiris' lore were well versed in agricultural cycles while priests who devoted themselves to Isis became experts in medicine; thus Ra, Osiris, and Isis extended from heaven all the way down into Egyptian bureaucracy!

As you learn more about these gods, you will discover they are not simply distant celestial figures; they serve as archetypes, life philosophies, and support systems for Egyptian life. What makes these ancient Egyptian deities truly fascinating aren't their magical abilities or epic tales but the layers of meaning they add to different aspects of Egyptian society - especially artifacts or artwork that date back centuries but remain relevant today; myths don't remain static but adapt with time as people believe them - so when staring at ancient Egyptian artifacts or art pieces remember: you are touching a treasure chest of knowledge rich with wisdom as well as timeless appeal!

4.1.2 River Gods and Goddesses: Guardians of the Nile

Join me now as we shift our focus from celestial to riverine! While Ra, Osiris, and Isis remain powerful figures of Egyptian mythology, let's not overlook those more in touch with Earth...or should I say water! Egypt's lifeblood the Nile River holds sacred its own pantheon of gods and goddesses dedicated to protecting it - these "guardian deities" even have stories to tell!

Hapi and Sobek stand as two gods who rule Egyptian legend. While Hapi may resemble "happy," its gifts gave Egyptians great joy. Imagine Hapi as the ultimate provider - the deity who ensures the Nile floods every year to deposit fertile soil onto fields. But this wasn't just any ordinary annual event: Hapi's presence ushered in dramatic rituals and festivities to mark this yearly occasion. Hapi was so essential to Egyptian life that he was often depicted as an androgynous male with female breasts and protruding belly, representing fertility and abundance. But there was more going on here - Hapi represented unity and balance by uniting male and female elements into one powerful deity, so you could say he multitasked as well! Now, that's something I call divine multitasking!

Sobek was an Egyptian god who represented all things Nile River--its wild side as well as its peaceful parts. Though commonly associated with destruction, Sobek wasn't just seen as a god. Sobek epitomized the duality of nature: revered yet feared as both guardian and predator. Sobek can appear to be both violent and insatiable creatures in some stories; on the other hand, in others he's worshiped as a protective deity to safeguard against dangers in the river, including attacks by crocodiles! Ancient Egyptians had temples dedicated to Sobek which included labyrinthine structures designed as den-like structures resembling his den. Now this may sound pretty intense! Nonetheless, this story of Sobek remains fascinating!

Do not give up now; we're only just scratching the surface! Egyptian river gods reflect the intricate relationships Egyptians had with their environment, reflecting natural forces such as creation, destruction and renewal - not one-note characters but multifaceted figures expressing this complexity through nuanced depictions representing creation, destruction and renewal in myth. You might already be asking yourself how these myths played a part in everyday Egyptian life - agriculture practices as well as art and architecture perhaps? Well hold tight! Because this narrative just gets richer from here on out!

Hapi and Sobek represent fertility and ferocity respectively, but there are other lesser-known deities who play equally captivating roles in aquatic myths, like Taweret and Khnum. Taweret often appears depicted as an pregnant hippopotamus standing on her hind legs for protection and fertility; Khnum was more commonly associated with protection. Taweret was revered among expectant mothers seeking protection for themselves or their newborns during gestation, making her the go-to deity. It seems as if all aspects of the Nile required multiple guardians; Taweret was there to give these intimate moments.

Khnum was revered in Egypt as the divine potter who created humans on his celestial wheel - like divine ceramics class! Khnum got his clay for this artistic endeavor directly from the Nile! Again, an illustration of just how closely related Nile gods were with creation in Egyptian mythology: this river god represented life itself!

But that's not all! These deities were not simply mythological figures in isolation from one another. Instead, they were seamlessly interwoven into Egyptian religious thought as an intricate tapestry woven by their gods' interweaved beings in a vast, divine ecosystem--one closely tied with natural ecosystems such as the Nile. Egyptians didn't view their gods as isolated figures but as interconnected beings within a vast, divine ecosystem--an environment which both fed crops as well as feeding imaginations of civilizations alike.

These ideas don't spring out of thin air; they have historical basis. Temples were constructed, rituals performed, hymns composed all in honor of these river deities; one could say the Nile was both physical and metaphysical to its environment; its myths and gods offer us an insight into Egyptian perception, interaction, and mythologizing of their surrounding environments.

As we began this journey by discussing sky gods and beings who tower above our world, it has become apparent that to truly comprehend Egyptian mythology one must immerse themselves in its depths and get their feet wet. River Gods and Goddesses offer insight into this intricate tapestry, not only offering stories but also lessons in balance, respect for nature and understanding the duality of existence. Trust me; these myths don't just flow one way--they explore every channel of Egyptian life and thought, nourishing a fertile field of human imagination that has thrived for millennia. Furthermore, my friend, this river doesn't end here; rather, it branches out into other stories while simultaneously branching off into myriad streams of interlinked mythology that you will soon come across on your exploration. Keep rowing; there's so much more out there waiting to be discovered!

4.2 Pyramids, Pharaohs, and the Realm of the Dead

So get ready, because we are about to embark on an incredible, mythical adventure through the ancient Egyptian world. When most people think of Egypt, pyramids come to mind--those massive structures with pointy tops that have fascinated people for millennia! While their physical beauty makes an impressionable statement about civilization's power and wisdom. Today we will delve into their mysteries and mysteries encased within these incredible architectural feats--so put on your imaginary explorer hat as we go!

This next part will explore how pyramids were more than just grand tombs for Pharaohs or monuments to their grandeur; they were testaments to an entire civilization's beliefs, ambitions, and cosmic understandings. From their alignment with stars to serving as gateways into afterlife realms - we will go further into how these iconic structures held more than mummies and treasure. They were and still serve as direct paths toward understanding Egypt's complicated web of myths around life, death, and what lies beyond.

So get ready as we take you on an in-depth journey as we explore what makes these ancient wonders not just feats of architectural brilliance, but also intricate tapestries of spiritual, cosmic and mythological meaning. Stay seated - it will be an exhilarating ride!

4.2.1 The Mythological Significance of Pyramids

Egypt would not be complete without its iconic pyramids dotting the landscape! Do they look like giant dice to you, but these grandiose triangular structures hold so much more significance - sacred architecture that testified to ancient civilization's cosmic outlook - let's unzip some of their mysteries!

Egyptian belief about pyramids centers on an idea called 'ka,' an aspect of soul that remains an indelible part of Egyptian belief. Physical life wasn't the end for ancient Egyptians - in fact it was just the opening act. After death came life after life - with an afterlife just waiting around the corner; preparation was key! A pyramid provided the perfect environment for this part two - perfectly aligning with heavens while carefully constructed for longevity to house their eternal home for their 'ka.

Ancient Egyptians were far ahead of their time when it came to stellar knowledge, evidenced by the Great Pyramid at Giza which is almost perfectly aligned with magnetic north. While impressive for engineering purposes, its alignment also stands as a powerful reminder of its spiritual meaning: its pointy tip seems poised as though ready to touch heaven itself!

Have you heard of the Orion Correlation Theory? This fascinating theory proposes that Giza pyramids are aligned astronomically with Orion's Belt stars--making this link even more remarkable because Orion was associated with Osiris, god of the afterlife. When combined together, this realization blew my mind! They not only serve as marvels of architecture but also serve as cosmic gateways into divine realms.

But we're not done yet! Pyramids served as massive repositories of religious texts etched onto their walls and providing spells, rituals, hymns and prayers designed to guide dead souls safely into the afterlife. Dubbed the Pyramid Texts by ancient scholars, these ancient inscriptions depict rituals performed and prayers spoken out loud to ensure safe passage into afterlife but they also hint at Egyptian worldview - these ancient inscriptions contain not just instructions but poetic verses that conveyed wisdom that connected earthly to celestial.

There's an immense significance in the actual building process itself! Constructing pyramids was no small task requiring unceasing cooperation among society as a whole to realize a shared vision, while simultaneously becoming an act of worship at this monumental scale in limestone and granite.

Think about it: workers weren't slaves but highly skilled laborers, often rotating three-month shifts. Many were deeply committed to serving their gods and Pharaoh's eternal life - which explains their dedication. Building these pyramids was like an act of devotion; an entire community coming together to construct something they may never benefit from personally. Now if that doesn't represent life's interconnection and our shared journey toward discovering the divine, I don't know what else could.

Consider too that their locations were carefully planned: these pyramids weren't randomly built - each site was carefully considered before selection. Many were strategically positioned near the western banks of the Nile, which symbolically signified life transitioning into death; when the sun set on those banks it marked this change as well. Pyramids served as gateways into eternity by connecting the mortal world with boundless expanses of eternity after death.

Not just Pharaohs got to experience afterlife fun; Egyptians as a whole believed in an afterlife journey known as the ka. Pyramids served as reminders that every soul had an eternal place in this cosmos, echoing society's hopes for eternal lives beyond mortality. Like an echo chamber for an entire culture longing for something grander; like saying to them "Look, I'm not just for my master king. I am here for us all to use, testament of something bigger, something infinite!"

Have we covered enough ground? From cosmic alignments to societal devotion, pyramids are steeped with mythological significance that extends far beyond their architectural marvel. Pyramids stand as powerful symbols of mankind's quest to understand our place in the cosmos and what lies beyond. Their lasting icon status comes from becoming timeless icons of humanity's eternal questions; not simply being tourist attractions but timeless reminders that challenge us to ponder things we don't yet know the answers for. They make for stunning photographic subjects for this reason alone!

4.2.2 Pharaohs as Living Gods: The Divine Rule

Pharaohs were considered more than mere monarchs: these powerful rulers were revered as living gods among mortals, making their jobs extremely demanding and immense pressure-inducing. Even their name, "Pharaoh," is full of symbolism derived from Ancient Egyptian 'Per-aa,' meaning Great House; being at the helm was no easy task!

Why were Pharaohs considered gods, you ask? The answer to your query lies within Egyptian concepts of Ma'at or cosmic order. Pharaohs were seen as earthly guardians of Ma'at who maintained balance and order within both mortal realm and divine cosmos by officiating grand ceremonies, performing sacred rituals, and generally keeping balance and order throughout both realms - officiating grand ceremonies, performing rituals sacred to their faith or just keeping Nile flowing as it should! Failing to maintain Ma'at could result in anything from famines to invasions! Pharaohs had to act like diplomats between nations as well as celestial entities! Talk about multitasking!

Horus, the falcon-headed god of kingship, inspired this marriage of royalty and divinity in Egypt's mythology. Pharaohs were believed to be human manifestations of Horus; therefore they wielded dual authority: over Egypt itself and over Osiris' realm in the afterlife - thus completing an amazing circle from god to man and back again! Pretty amazing?

Now let's get down to details: the Pharaohs' divine status was evident in various customs and traditions that ranged from their dress code to language use. They donned special headcloths called Nemes and

Uraeus (cobra), symbols unique to themselves and the gods; their names were often enclosed within an elongated loop called a serekh or cartouche to signify their godly lineage; these rulers weren't simply members of royal families but celestial beings with lineages stretching all the way back to those represented by these rulers themselves!

Are everyone aware of their divine status as Pharaoh? Generally, yes. Belief in their divinity was embedded within society itself, with hymns, prayers, and monumental inscriptions all extolling his divine status in order to boost his authority. But it should be noted that being god king didn't give Pharaoh carte blanche when it came to acting at will: their divine status came with moral and spiritual obligations such as justiciable governance, ritualistic offerings, military prowess.

Akhenaten was an exceptional Pharaoh who used his power for revolutionary change by instituting monotheism - rejecting traditional pantheism to proclaim Aten, the sun disk god, as supreme god and thus shifting his role subtly yet noticeably within Egypt's religion and society at large. While his reforms were eventually undone by successor kings, Akhenaten's reign stands as proof of how dynamically Pharaonic divine roles could adapt with time.

Now if you're curious as to whether queens enjoyed any slice of divine glory in Ancient Egypt, prepare to be delighted. Queenship in its divine sense was closely tied with Isis' role as archetype of perfect wife and motherhood, making powerful figures like Hatshepsut, Nefertiti, and Cleopatra not just shadow figures of their royal spouses or fathers but rather powerful forces themselves; often attributing godlike traits and responsibilities; Hatshepsut even went further by wearing false beard, traditionally reserved only for Pharaohs so as to emphasize her authority or divine mandate from Isis! These women weren't simply sitting around but rather shaping history and mythology with each move they made.

Switching gears slightly, we will explore the ceremonies that cemented Pharaohs' divine stature; in particular the Heb Sed festival. This ritual was similar to an energy recharge ritual and sought to renew their energies and renew ties to their gods. Pharaohs raced, offered sacrifices and participated in complex rituals during this festival with rich symbolism as part of this divine renewal ritual; these were believed to renew vitality while reset cosmic order--it was like nature's version of an update: necessary and transformative!

Zooming out further, the idea that Pharaohs were god-kings wasn't simply an insular belief but also used as a diplomatic tactic. Letters exchanged between Pharaohs and foreign rulers often contained epithets highlighting his divine nature as an effective form of soft power that further cemented Egyptian society as being not just another kingdom but led by an actual god.

Phew! What an eventful journey! To sum it all up: the role of Pharaoh as god was not an ornamental title but instead became part of Egyptian mythology, politics, and daily life. From Horus to Ma'at and divine queens like Nefertiti, as well as radical reformers such as Radical Reformer Ahmose IV; their godly status changed constantly over time - so when viewing an Egyptian statue or painting featuring one, remember: you are looking into someone believed by ancient Egyptians to stand alongside god himself or herself! So next time when looking at such artwork depicting Pharaohs this way: you aren't looking into simply another ruler but rather gazing into someone believed to have stood equal with god himself! So next time when gazing upon an Egyptian statue or painting featuring one, remember, you are gazing into someone believed by ancient Egyptians themselves!

4.2.3 Journey Through the Afterlife: The Book of the Dead

At first, when you heard "The Book of the Dead," it may sound like something out of a horror movie. Not so fast; instead it is an anthology, compilation and guidebook to navigating the complex highways and byways of ancient Egyptian afterlife - not an afterlife like you might expect - with many trials, tribulations and heart-wrenching journeys waiting after death; using The Book of the Dead as their travel guide through all manners of spiritual realm.

But let's delve deeper and understand its origins: "The Book of the Dead" was not one time but an accumulation of spells, prayers, and rituals gathered over centuries by what became known as "Coffin Texts," inscriptions carved into coffins to assist departed souls on their journeys into afterlife. Over time these spells became less exclusive to royalty but accessible to anyone with enough money for expensive papyrus to purchase copies - after all even afterlife had its luxuries?

Families could select which spells and sections they wanted included, creating their own "Build-Your-Own-Afterlife-Manual." Families could customize it according to what was important to them - remembering names (something important even after death!), not getting eaten by crocodiles (seriously!), and more besides. Some spells even assisted you with taking on various animal forms like birds or snakes to adapt to various landscapes you would visit; you could imagine your soul taking shape as a heron to glide over an celestial river - pretty cool?

Now that you have your customized Book of the Dead and bid farewell to mortal life, what lies ahead in the afterlife is an intoxicating prospect; your first stop should be Ma'at, the goddess of truth and justice, where your soul will be judged against her Feather for any sin committed during life - too many and your fate becomes decidedly grim if not. Should it pass the test? Osiris welcomes you into his Field of Reeds as an eternal paradise where speech and actions can help win over gods through Book of Dead spells prepared you well enough before this step - providing guidance so your words and actions won't offend her/him/her/him for an eternal paradise await.

Refresh yourself now as what follows will explore the Egyptian concept of afterlife, with different realms, interactions with gods and goddesses, and daily life of an Egyptian soul in paradise - everything from food eaten in paradise to animal-headed gods who may assist or hinder on its path - will all play into its understanding.

Ready to dive deeper? Great! Let's delve deeper into the Egyptian concept of afterlife. The paradisiacal Field of Reeds doesn't simply replicate your earthly life - rather, it serves as a reflection of all your desires and comforts in an eternal setting. Imagine feasting on celestial versions of your favorite foods and engaging in activities you once loved most in life, yet without mortal constraints limiting you. In the Field of Reeds, these activities no longer seem laborious; rather they become joyful adventures reimagined without physical strain or limitations. The Book of the Dead provides advice for living well after death - not only getting there but thriving once there. It provides advice on how to communicate with gods and spirits so you are accepted by them all; think of it like ancient Egyptian Miss Manners for postmortem socializing!

Egyptians believed in cycles and eternity; your soul could travel between realms as an ancestral guide or spirit and even be reborn into another body. Spells in the Book of the Dead provided ways for it to do this; acting like passports between dimensions for it to remain an active, evolving entity forever part of a cosmic dance between life, death, and rebirth.

4.3 Deciphering the Hieroglyphs: Texts and Spells

Hieroglyphs aren't simply decorative forms of writing - they contain alphabetic, syllabic and logographic elements crammed into each squiggle and bird shape; imagine ancient Egyptians jam-packing their entire civilization's knowledge into every squiggle or bird shape - buckle up! We are diving deep into these symbols, syntaxes and stupendously complex world that lay out these texts and spells

Imagine this: as an ancient scribe trained in the sacred art of writing, your inkwell is full, your reed pen sharpened, and you are about to start on an elaborate Book of the Dead for a recently deceased noble. Your writing won't just be letters; each hieroglyph you inscribe onto its surface holds both literal and symbolic significance - any misplacement could prove disastrously fatal!

Not surprisingly, symbols written in the Book of the Dead don't appear uniformly either! Instead, their direction varies depending on the context and object they adorn, often facing left-to-right, right-to-left, or top-to-bottom! Interestingly enough, sometimes their direction even helps clarify meaning; multitasking at its finest! So you see: A scroll from the Book of the Dead is more than just words on papyrus; it is an intricate narrative that requires decoding rather than simply reading!

Scribes had their work cut out for them when it came to crafting spells! You'll find spells written with various degrees of complexity to meet the client's specific needs; wealthy clients could afford more elaborate spells (think buying the deluxe edition with extra tips and VIP routes). Spells covered everything from protection and sustenance to knowledge and power; each spell was composed using hieroglyphs carefully chosen to invoke specific energies or outcomes--it was like having a recipe book full of spells designed specifically to address various life scenarios or results!

Hieroglyphic texts and spells offer unique glimpses into ancient Egyptian understandings of the cosmos.

Imagine that! There was even a symbol for "infinity!" Hieroglyphs representing abstract ideas like eternity, cycles and duality were embedded into these spells, giving us insight into their sophisticated and holistic worldview. The ingenuity and nuance of their writing system speaks volumes of their progressivism and advanced worldview.

So when you look upon those intricate symbols, keep this in mind: when gazing upon these ancient forms of writing, keep in mind that you are peering into the minds of a people who saw everything as profoundly interrelated; every spell was seen as part of an ever-expanding cosmic web and every hieroglyph was just another droplet in existence; their writing wasn't simply writing but weaving fabric of metaphysical realm - the Book of Dead's hieroglyphs were its compass, map and terrain all at once!

Aren't hieroglyphs mind-boggling to contemplate? With their vast reservoir of meaning, philosophy, and practical wisdom distilled into such obscure symbols? Hieroglyphs were the backbone of ancient Egyptian afterlife as an orchestrated symphony of interlinked realities; when you encounter one today it's worth pausing and reflecting; each symbol holds meanings just waiting to be unlocked by analysis. When you encounter an elegantly etched ankh or Eye of Horus symbol, take time out and consider its hidden secrets - its meaning awaits exploration!

4.3.1 The Rosetta Stone and the Mystery of Hieroglyphs

Hieroglyphs may seem hard to break through, so let's discuss one key that opened them: the Rosetta Stone is the literal key that unlocked ancient Egyptian symbols and scripts. Not just any rock; the Rosetta Stone is not simply one language--it speaks three! Known for being written in Ancient Greek, Demotic, and Hieroglyphs--this notice from King Ptolemy V was sent across three scripts at once--ancient Greek, Demotic, and Hieroglyphs--it was written as bureaucratic notice about King Ptolemy V who ruled Egypt at that time.

What makes this stone truly special isn't what its message says but how it says it three different times! - like sending three texts simultaneously saying the same message- three different times: sending three separate messages saying the same thing in different formats- it was like sending multiple text, tweet and handwritten letter all saying the same message multiple ways- this stone communicated three different times! That would be like sending three separate texts, tweet and handwritten letter all saying the same message... which would mean different things depending on who read it and then sent three separate forms of communication more effective?

By 1799 when it was found near Rosetta (now Rashid in modern-day Egypt), no one could read hieroglyphs -

mysterious symbols written centuries earlier that had long since vanished into history. Thanks to the Rosetta Stone however, scholars could compare Greek which many educated people knew how to read with Hieroglyphics as they struggled alongside each other - almost like someone saying, 'Enough already; here's your cheat sheet."

Why did it take so long to decode hieroglyphics with the Rosetta Stone in hand? Well, these scripts are far from transparent. Their structure can be just as complex as that of a Swiss watch! Think of Demotic as ancient Egyptians street slang filled with colloquialisms and shortcuts; while Ancient Greek was considered the language of rulers and bureaucracy. Understanding hieroglyphics requires understanding concepts across three distinct dialects each with its own nuance, idioms, and context.

Deciphering the Rosetta Stone was no simple task; it required mental triathlon and four-dimensional chess. French scholar Jean-Francois Champollion finally cracked its code in 1822 after years of dedicated effort; even so, this monumental task took him years as it required him to be an expert in languages, history, cultures and phonetics of languages that hadn't been spoken for centuries!

He experienced his "a-ha!" moment when he realized some hieroglyphs could be read phonetically--meaning they represented sounds rather than ideas or objects. He began studying cartouches containing royal names as possible sources for phonetic glyphs; eventually it clicked; for instance, King Ptolemy's cartouche contained symbols which when spoken aloud would sound just like "Ptolemy." Not only was decipherment being achieved here; resurrection was occurring! A dead language had come back to life!

Imagine trying to assemble a jigsaw puzzle without knowing which pieces belong. Without even the box as reference, imagine the magnitude of Champollion's achievement - not simply academic hoop-jumping but detective work of the highest order!

Unpacking the Rosetta Stone was like peeling an onion: each layer revealed more depth and complexity than before, from scripts telling similar tales but from different cultures or time periods; to hieroglyphs that both inspired and baffled for centuries before Champollion deciphered them and opened a door into ancient civilization's beliefs, history, and daily lives- it was like landing on the moon!

Champollion's breakthrough had far-reaching ramifications across academia and society alike, significantly altering our understanding of ancient Egyptian culture. But let's be realistic; once Champollion found the basic phonetic key for hieroglyphs, further questions arose regarding their development over time, adaptation for writing monumental inscriptions, religious texts, administrative documents etc. The Rosetta Stone was simply the starting point; not its endpoint.

Researchers grappled with unique difficulties when studying hieroglyphs. Without vowels, emphasis, or punctuation as we know it today, how could one comprehend its subtleties? Furthermore, hieroglyphs were more than mere symbols: they played an essential part of religious rituals and beliefs. More than mere letters they represented living beings filled with mythological and cultural meaning - with their initial scribes serving not just as clerks but as priests charged with protecting God's divine word.

But let's backtrack a bit. Remember how Demotic and Greek were also on the stone? Their interaction wasn't simple - each language had its own grammar, vocabulary and stylistic quirks that required Champollion and scholars who followed him to switch effortlessly between linguistic frameworks while respecting individual idiosyncrasies; for instance Greek text had subtleties that neither Demotic nor hieroglyphic versions could capture, like reading Shakespearean sonnets, contemporary novels, rap lyrics lyric lyric lyric lyric all at the same time - no small feat at all!

Do not underestimate the geopolitical aspect of all this either. When the Rosetta Stone was discovered during Napoleon's campaign in Egypt, it quickly became a symbol of colonial rivalry. Britain and France vied to own it, each sensing its immense value to knowledge advancement. Eventually it wound up at the British Museum, raising profound issues related to cultural heritage, ownership rights and archaeology--issues still fiercely debated today.

What was Rosetta Stone's takeaway? Not simply decoding hieroglyphs; rather it launched an interdisciplinary revolution that blurred lines among linguistics, history, archaeology and cultural studies and forced scholars to adopt more holistic approaches in their studies. Furthermore, its discovery not only revealed hieroglyphs; rather it demonstrated how interwoven our human stories are. By deciphering every inscription from ancient societies which have had such an enormous influence on today's globalized world.

One thing is for certain: the Rosetta Stone was more than just a slab of rock; it served as a gateway into another world, an intellectual landmark, and an inspiring testament of human creativity and ingenuity. So next time someone mentions the Rosetta Stone, know it isn't just about hieroglyphs - rather, its significance lies in language's power to conceal, reveal, and transcend time and space - thus keeping its mystery alive today.

4.3.2 Magical Spells and Rituals in Everyday Life

When we think of magic, our minds often go straight to elaborate ceremonies and esoteric incantations accompanied by elaborate ceremonies or the waving of wands. But in ancient Egyptian society, magic--known locally as Heka"--was an integral part of daily life, just as natural as breathing or drinking from the Nile. Pharaohs and commoners alike used magical practices both ceremonially as well as everyday for everyday tasks; therefore why shouldn't we shed preconceptions and explore this fascinating universe where divine energies ran through daily life?

Let's first consider the power dynamics surrounding magic. Contrary to modern assumptions of separation between religion and magic, Heka was seen as an elemental divine force embedded into Egyptian spiritual culture and thought - its creator being Atum - and its reach spanned all corners of society - not limited to elite members or the ruling classes alone. Practice was democratized too: anyone from Pharaohs, soldiers or fisherman could tap into its powers - there even existed specialists like "Hekau", well versed in magical texts and rituals who were well versed on how best to utilize Heka in their work - similar to modern-day spiritual consulting services!

Imagine yourself as an Ancient Egyptian farmer whose herd has fallen ill, and your only option is calling on your local Hekau! He may use incantations, physical rituals and perhaps some talismans to rid your herd of disease - this might sound like folklore today; yet back then this was standard procedure! In reality though, what we now consider medicine was often combined with religion or magic and spells were sometimes included among therapeutic repertoire - each element contributing their unique energy towards creating effective treatments - making holistic medicine not so new-age as some might assume!

Fascinating was how magic played a role in managing interpersonal relationships. If you find yourself feeling attracted to someone but can't express them properly, ancient Egyptian magic is there for you: love spells were legitimate tools of expression cast using amulets or papyri. However, these spells weren't without ethical dilemmas: society would often debate between harmless love spells and those that crossed over into manipulation or coercion - much like how our current discussions about consent have played out over the centuries. And let's not even touch curses or hexes! These dark sides of Heka were equally pervasive but more so in ancient Egyptian society!

Heka's beauty (or mystery) lay in its intricate cosmology. Spells and rituals were often deeply connected to Egyptian "Ma'at," or cosmic balance, making magic not simply to meet individual needs but to maintain equilibrium of the universe itself. An effective spell was one that aligned with Ma'at principles by not just fulfilling an individual desire but contributing towards greater good; even as you cast spells to ensure a fruitful harvest you were also partaking in God's act of maintaining cosmic equilibrium!

Who could forget the Weighing of the Heart ceremony in the Afterlife? Magic transcended life and death, and this spell, typically found in funerary texts, was intended to ensure that a deceased's heart wouldn't testify against them when their soul passed into the afterlife. These spells served as forms of cosmic advocacy; petitioning, pleading or coaxing the gods into maintaining an accepting attitude toward their dead was all part of keeping a positive perception about them in heaven.

Magic in ancient Egypt was far more than simple conjuring; it was an intricate body of knowledge spanning science, religion and philosophy. Egyptians lived magic - each incantation being part of Heka's power; every amulet an anchor in an elaborate network of divine relationships - every ritual part of an ever-expanding fabric of reality.

So far, you've probably gained a solid understanding of Heka's impact on ancient Egyptian life - from health and romance to justice and cosmic harmony. Now let's focus on the nitty-gritty: everyday magical practices themselves. Understanding these details not only enhances academic curiosity; understanding them sheds light on psychology, aspirations and fear within societies that flourished millennia ago - it makes the whole subject all the more captivating!

Let's delve deeper into amulets, or wearable spells, which were similar to pendants today but with special meaning for their wearers. Each amulet was handcrafted of materials selected specifically for their magical properties and bore geometric designs specific to its use as an amulet; wearing one was like becoming an antenna tuned into specific cosmic frequencies: from Ankh amulets for eternal life and stability through Djed pillars to Eye of Horus pieces crafted for protection; amulets could even be tailored specifically to align with an individual's magical needs, kind of like custom spirituality for these devices!

Magic was not limited to physical objects in Ancient Egypt; its roots ran deep into their language as words themselves were seen as potent magical tools. Etymologists take note: Egyptians considered the act of naming as a form of creation - to bring something into existence, define its essence, and exert some level of control over it. No wonder then that names of gods were often kept a closely guarded secret only invoked under extreme conditions (think Voldemort-level taboos!).

Let's also explore Heka in society norms and laws, beyond spell casting alone. When legal systems were inadequate or found wanting, individuals often turned to magical means as an alternative means of justice. Spell jars (execration texts) would often contain the names of enemies or wrongdoers etched upon their interior walls before being ceremoniously broken to cause harm or bad luck; although this practice might seem harsh in modern parlance it provides fascinating insight into an alternative justice system that was widely practiced - including state officials who participated before military campaigns to subdue enemies before battle began!

At first glance, Ancient Egyptian life may appear filled with superstitions; however, this was actually an organized form of spirituality with rules and regulations, checks and balances built-in that operated more like an empirical system than simply faith; spells were revised regularly, new amulets created, and magical techniques were recorded and documented like today's tech industry R&D department.

Let us not forget the scholars and intellectuals within magic; those practitioners who were also theoreticians. Their world was one filled with papyri that served as academic journals describing new advances, outlining which spells were more effective than others and debating ethical questions related to magical practices. Such texts were strictly protected as they passed from master to apprentice - often carefully hidden away from outsiders looking in.

4.3.3 The Book of the Dead and Other Sacred Texts

Just the name conjures an air of mysticism. However, let us be clear here--this wasn't one book but rather an assortment of spells, prayers and hymns which could be personalized according to an individual's journey through afterlife. Individualized copies were even created just for those who could afford them; truly VIP treatment in hell!

Texts like The Book of the Dead held immense spiritual and worldbuilding significance, not only providing spiritual guidance but also creating vivid world-building descriptions of landscapes and challenges souls would face when entering afterlife; providing clues, shortcuts and hints through labyrinthine tests set up by gods, demons, or cosmic balances that served as road maps towards salvation. Each spell served as a key or hack to bypass difficulties set up by these cosmic balances and gods.

But how did people use this book? It wasn't like a manual you'd tuck away in your coffin; rather, portions were often inscribed on tomb walls or written on papyrus scrolls close to mummies as reminders on how to navigate their spiritual realm. Sometimes excerpts were even inscribed onto bandages of the deceased--sort of like spiritual Post-it Notes to help navigate spirituality with participatory spirituality at its finest! It was interactive spirituality at its finest!

"The Book of the Dead" may receive much media coverage, but it was far from the only sacred text for Egyptians. Other texts such as Coffin Texts and Pyramid Texts served distinct but interlinked roles; Pharaohs used these precursors of "The Book of the Dead", known as Pyramid Texts, as VIP lounge access cards to enter Egyptian afterlife via pyramid walls carved directly by them; some scholars even speculate that these texts served ritual magic that affected both deceased and living world.

Texts such as the Book of the Dead were far ahead of their time; raising questions that continue to preoccupy philosophers today. Issues such as existence and nonexistence, soul nature and cosmic justice were urgent matters that demanded immediate consideration and understanding; almost as though ancient Egyptians were engaged in a grand metaphysical dialogue through spells, hymns and magic words which added layers to its discourse.

But that would be inaccurate; sacred texts played an integral role in everyday Egyptian lives as well. Quotes from sacred texts would often find their way into popular hymns, local lore and even everyday phrases - like verses from a holy book turning into popular idioms used daily by citizens of ancient Egypt. Furthermore, ancient Egypt's sacred texts weren't just tomes gathering dust on some shelf but were living, breathing entities integrated into society as whole - accessible not just to elite noblemen but to anyone willing to engage them - be they nobleman or farmer alike.

But much like modern software, the "Book of Dead" underwent revisions over time as society changed, adding or subtracting spells based on cultural nuances of that era and age. Revisions also came about from religious, political, and environmental changes; after all these texts were created during an era when empires rose and fell, gods were dethroned or canonized, landscapes underwent massive shifts - it's remarkable to think how these texts managed to remain relevant, adaptive and indispensable throughout this long stretch of time! It truly amazes us!

Spells and incantations written down may appear like mere superstition, but remember they were painstakingly researched from various scholarly traditions. Far from being random or random-seeming, formulas were precise as Egyptians believed the universe operated according to Ma'at (cosmic balance), with every utterance needing to respect this delicate equilibrium. That is why many spells included redundancies for backup power failure - much like backup generators today!

Let us also acknowledge the artistry of ancient texts written down as written words; be they inscribed on tomb walls or written on papyrus scrolls, their visual aspects were equally significant. Spells didn't just exist in words alone; they took form through illustrations and hieroglyphics as part of the spell itself. These details weren't just decorative features; they played an essential part in its power. Text and image were inextricably interwoven; each adding its own layer of meaning and potency to one another. For example, consider an instruction on how to become a bird in the afterlife; its accompanying illustration would not depict just any old bird but instead one with significant symbolic and cultural associations like falcon or heron which were considered sacred animals.

Ancient Egyptians understood a sacred text to be more than just a book; rather, it was an immersive multimedia experience engaging readers on many levels through text, images and ritual.

What happens when empires fall and new cultures and languages arise? Egypt's sacred texts did not simply fade with time; instead they created an everlasting legacy that continued to influence generations long after their last hieroglyphic was inked. Not only were these works crucial in developing Abrahamic religions; they were also instrumental in sparking Renaissance magic revival through Hermeticism revivalist movements such as Renaissance Hermeticism. Even today as scholars translate and interpret ancient works they continue reshaping how we view religion, philosophy, and human thought!

Boook 5 with Epic Bonus 1: Japanese Mythology

5.1 Understanding Kami: The Divine in Everything

Let us now embark upon an incredible adventure as we travel across Japan's ethereal landscapes, where mythology swirls like mist over mountains. At its center lies Kami - an abstract concept which often leaves Western theologians scratching their heads; not quite god nor spirit yet somehow infusing everyday experiences with an aura of divinity.

Kami in Shinto, Japan's indigenous religion, can be an intricate and mysterious concept that is sometimes difficult for even experienced mythology enthusiasts to grasp. But Kami is fascinating because it embraces everything--be it deities, ancestors, animals or natural phenomena such as waterfalls and volcanoes--from deities and demigods to natural phenomena like waterfalls or volcanoes! Even its name, which derives from Japanese words meaning 'above or superior,' encompasses something greater than human existence while simultaneously fundamentally interwed with human existence - an aspect which comes back around time! That first surprise about Kami: its sheer presence.

Take a step back, however, and consider its historical evolution. Early Japanese myths as recorded in texts such as Kojiki and Nihon Shoki provide us with glimpses into how Kami served not just religious but also cultural, social and even political functions in Japanese society. Ruling families claimed descent from Kami, thus providing justification for their authority, while clans paid their respects to certain Kamis by creating shrines and festivals in their honor. Syncretism provides an intriguing glimpse of how divine and human realms were not distinct; they coexisted on a continuum. This contrasts sharply with many Western mythologies in which gods typically exist separately from humanity only occasionally interfering in human affairs.

Do you find it puzzling that a single term encompasses such an expansive list of entities and phenomena? Don't fret: Japan's intricate relationship between nature, ancestry and community embodied by Kami is well known - everything interconnects - there's no strict dualism between good and evil or sacred and profane; instead it functions more like a divine ecosystem with each component playing their part from grand gods tasked with creation/destruction to rice deities who ensure bountiful harvests/...

Are You A Fan of Japanese Animation/Manga? If so, then you may recognize the subtle ties between humanity and divinity in Japanese animation or manga. Characters often encounter ancient shrines, speak with spirit animals or find out that they're related to celestial beings - all hallmarks of divinity in their lives that don't just appear suddenly out there somewhere distant but are integrated into daily living experiences. It is an artistic reflection of an embedded worldview where divinity exists as part of daily living experience rather than far off in some distant heaven but as part of daily living life - where divinity resides among us a part of everyday living experiences!

Understanding Kami can be like trying to catch water with one hand; it slips through easily. Yet that is its beauty: it challenges us to think outside our preconceived boxes and engage with God more directly and personally. Ancient Egypt encouraged us to look up, outward and upward for spiritual guidance; Kami encourages us instead to discover extraordinary moments all around and within ourselves. But how should one approach Kami, you might ask? And how has this understanding influenced rituals, folklore, and the moral fabric of Japan? As we dig deeper, each layer that's peeled back reveals even more layers - almost like peeling back an onion--or rather more accurately--like unwrapping a celestial Matryoshka Doll of interlinked wonders!

As we gain greater insight into Kami, one of the first things to recognize is that its significance runs far deeper than just an abstract philosophical concept - it has become part of Japanese daily life and culture itself. From grand ceremonies at iconic shrines like Ise Jingu to humble roadside altars, spirituality mingles with everyday life at every level of existence. Imagine this: a Japanese fisherman casting his net into the ocean without first paying his respects to Kami of the sea for an abundant catch; or an urban Tokyo resident stopping off at a Shinto shrine on their way to work while seemingly out of place amid digital billboards and skyscrapers nearby. These instances illustrate how Kami plays such an integral part in Japanese history and daily life alike.

But don't make the mistake of mistaking Kami for some unchanging concept frozen in time - like its tides, it has changed and evolved over time. Buddhism arrived in Japan during the 6th century AD with its own pantheon of deities and celestial beings; rather than uprooting native beliefs it created an intriguing form of syncretism where Buddhist figures were integrated into the Kami framework. This resulted in a beautiful spiritual landscape where Shinto shrines and Buddhist temples coexisted together peacefully alongside one another - something rarely seen nowadays in modern societies with religious binaries.

Are You Visualizing Kami as Nothing But Tranquility? Hold onto Your Hats! These Kami are more than gentle spirits--they also possess powerful, intimidating aspects. Take for instance the Kami that accompany natural disasters such as Raijin (God of Thunder and Lightning) or Fujin (God of Wind). While not evil themselves, these manifestations of nature deserve respect and reverence just like their more sedate counterparts do; thus appeasing and honoring these Kami helps avoid their wrath - again reflecting nature's duality between creation and destruction within their figures!

At its heart, Kami's beauty lies in its radical inclusivity: inviting everyone to participate in its divine realm while breaking down barriers of sanctity to create an almost democratic spiritual experience. Consider this: in what other theology system do rocks and trees receive the same regard as celestial beings? Where else in worldview does a humble rice deity stand equal with an intimidating dragon god? Kami serves as an important reminder that everything has intrinsic worth that should be recognized.

Why should someone thousands of miles away care about Kami? Because she offers us an insightful lesson in seeing heaven in every particle of sand - something poet William Blake wrote of doing himself. Her tale challenges us to see that our surroundings are alive with divinity, magic and immense potential; breaking out of anthropocentric viewpoints to imagine a cosmology consisting of interconnecting relationships instead of hierarchies.

5.2 The Three Sacred Treasures of Japan

Plunge into Japanese mythology, and you'll soon come upon an intriguing trio: the Three Sacred Treasures of Japan - also known as Imperial Regalia. We're talking here about artifacts of cosmic significance such as Kusanagi-no-Tsurugi's sword, Yata no Kagami mirror, and Yasakani no Magatama jewel; each represents something important to Japanese identity such as Mount Fuji or cherry blossoms of spring. So buckle up, because we're going deep into understanding these relics' essence! So strap yourself up! We're about to examine what makes these relics tick - why these treasures are so iconic.

Let's begin this discussion with Kusanagi-no-Tsurugi, the sword that's shrouded in divine mystery and boasts an unforgettable history. Its origins are truly extraordinary! Legend holds that Susanoo discovered this sword from Yamata no Orochi, an eight-headed serpent he defeated to save a maiden. But its origin alone does not make this tale worthy of admiration; its story itself makes for fascinating reading. Japanese culture views swords as entities possessing spirit. Not just tools of war, these revered objects come complete with histories and personalities of their own. Kusanagi-no-Tsurugi symbolizes valor and warrior spirit, making it an emblem of Japan's imperial ceremony even though its true form is never displayed publicly - its sacred status prevents this. Instead, an exact replica is used instead - adding further mystery to its existence.

Let's now move onto discussing Yata no Kagami, or the sacred mirror. This mirror stands as a powerful symbol of wisdom and truth born out of another high-stakes mythological story. At one point, Amaterasu had taken to withdrawing into a cave, plunging the world into darkness. To lure her out again, various gods used divine magic - including Yata no Kagami! It played an important role in that celestial intervention! Amaterasu used it to see her reflection, which in turn aroused her curiosity and led to her leaving the cave, thus returning light back into the world - now that's an effective mirror! Like swords, Yata no Kagami should never be put on public display but kept away safely as a reminder of wisdom and self-reflection's value and reverence.

Yasakani no Magatama, the beguiling yet significant comma-shaped jewel is both bewitching and meaningful. This treasure represents benevolence and fertility; often related to cyclicality of life and reproduction; used as talismans, this gem's power extends even farther - often used during rituals to connect humans and gods through its symbols of magick or spiritual forces that pervade existence; acting as a conduit between earthly life and divine realms, similar to its sword and mirror counterparts counterparts!

Why do these three artifacts resonate so powerfully with Japanese society? Are their mythological roots responsible, or is there more to consider? Well, don't answer that yet as we have only just scratched the surface of what these treasures contribute to Japanese culture. Take note: They are not simply isolated relics; together, they represent what it means to be Japanese: an inclusive view that links divine with mortal, past with present, myth with reality and myth to reality.

What makes the Three Sacred Treasures of Japan most fascinating is their connection to modern Japan - they don't just represent old stories that have since faded, but play an integral role in shaping its cultural and political fabric. The Emperor serves as an embodiment of Japan's unity and receives these items through an elaborate yet secretive ceremony, passing them from generation to generation. Japanese citizens might never actually see these treasures themselves, yet their collective reverence unites a collective consciousness. These items don't just belong to another time; they remain part of Japan's national identity in spite of technological progress and modernity - think of them as King Arthur's Excalibur with three times as much spiritual depth.

Now, it is natural to wonder why these treasures have endured through centuries and dynasties; their mythological allure as well as philosophical underpinnings are no doubt part of their appeal. Japanese culture is known for emphasizing balance and harmony, and each treasure in their culture embodies one or more virtues such as valor, wisdom or generosity. Like the best haikus, the treasures serve a purpose and place, contributing to aesthetic and ethical harmony. Their arrangement embodies the Japanese concept of 'wa' (peace and harmony); when taken together they make an ideal triplet that represents this balance, representing virtues essential for leading an enlightened life and rule.

And to add further mystery and suspense, let's add to their allure by discussing their hidden nature. Remember, none of these treasures are available for public viewing - which gives each object an air of mystery that beguiles us into reflecting upon its symbolic virtues rather than focussing on physical forms alone. Hideous places give their power away as reminders to us all of how powerfully their message truly resonates within each of us - which lies at their very heart!

What makes these treasures even more fascinating is their widespread appearance across history, literature and pop culture, solidifying their lore among different media and generations. Noh plays from ancient Japan have inspired modern manga depictions that feature their presence; from 14th-century Taiheiki chronicles to modern anime adaptations depicting them, these timeless artifacts serve as living reminders of a culture's values that remains deep-seated yet constantly changing.

As we step back and assess this journey, let's pause to take in all that these treasures represent - they go far beyond mere history or culture! Mythologies are living, breathing symbols of national identity that can serve as guides for our collective lives and behaviors - complex yet harmonious, ancient yet evergreen. When we unraveled their mythos, we did more than explore legends of gods and heroes - we gained insight into a living, breathing nation's soul. As we've traveled deep into Japanese culture and its ethical foundations, we should now have a greater appreciation of what it means to be human in an unpredictable and multidimensional world. But stay tuned; Japanese mythology holds many more surprises for us to uncover; these three artifacts are just the tip of the iceberg!

5.3 From Izanami and Izanagi: Creation Myths

They're like Adam and Eve in Judeo-Christian tradition or Gaia and Uranus in Greek mythology - powerful divine beings who represent Japan's version of creation myths. Like them or not, their story not only depicts birth but also of love lost along the way and life after death.

Imagine this: an empty and formless celestial realm ready to witness its first act of existence. Izanami and Izanagi are given Ame-no-Nuboko jeweled spears by God as part of their divine mission: creating something out of nothingness. So they do what's obvious to create something from nothingness: dip Ame-no-Nuboko into the celestial ocean with little ripple, until one drop falls from it hardening into Onogoro island - seemingly straightforward... But just wait... Things get much more complex from here on out...

After arriving on this newly formed island, a unique love story unfolds that you won't find in modern rom-coms. Izanami and Izanagi decide to get married, using ritualistic means similar to how gods of creation work: by circling a pillar, invoking incantations and eventually giving birth to islands through divine love! Japan itself was created this way, from wind gods and mountains god's right through to gods who represent mud! Talk about productive relationships!

But all is not well in this heavenly tale; life and death exist simultaneously, leading to tragedy when Izanami dies while giving birth to Kagutsuchi, the fire god. Grieved and incensed, Izanagi descends into Yomi (the underworld) in search of Izanami only to discover her lesser than divine state: decomposed and ruling over Yomi's realm of the dead while longing to return - showing an intricate interplay of life and death as she yearns to return; life itself contains both light and darkness encased within its pages!

It is this duality that pervades Japanese mythology, with Izanami and Izanagi acting as an embodiment of that duality throughout their tale. Their story doesn't just revolve around creation; it also features destruction. Their tale forms the cornerstone for many recurring themes in Japanese mythology and Shinto philosophy such as purification, cycles of death and rebirth and harmonious balances of opposites woven throughout this narrative - serving as an exemplar that sets precedents for generations of gods and humans to navigate similar complexities!

As one can easily imagine, this myth forms the bedrock of Japanese spiritual and cultural identity. Elements of their tale still resonate today in Shinto rituals, shrine layout, and how people view life and death - making this not just folklore; this tale packs philosophical concepts within its narrative fabric - this story offers layers upon layers of symbolism, morality and existential questioning that make up its entirety and make it an indispensable tool in understanding Japan as a culture.

As is so often the case in literature and art, the story of Izanami and Izanagi doesn't end neatly with a bow. Instead, when Izanagi flees from Yomi upon realizing he can no longer bring Izanami back, he initiates an iconic purification ritual which sets in motion Shinto practices. By bathing in the sea to rid himself of Yomi's pollution and purification rituals such as bathing to rid himself of pollution of Yomi in Yomi; from this single act alone new gods spring forth out of each droplet of water droplet; symbolic yet transformative and testaments to how every ending leads to something new beginning - even from decay comes new life from its ashes!

This particular motif resonates in numerous aspects of Japanese culture, from Oharae--where people purify themselves through similar rituals--to "Mono no Aware," an aesthetic principle that recognizes beauty in everything that passes away; like cultural DNA it keeps reappearing through practices, thoughts and beliefs.

No less noteworthy are Izanami and Izanagi's siblings and children: Amaterasu the Sun Goddess, Tsukuyomi the Moon God and Susanoo, the Storm God to name just a few. Not simply additional characters in a celestial drama but manifestations of natural forces held sacred by ancient Japanese, such as Amaterasu's retreat into a cave leading to darkness - an allegory for her importance that anticipates modern ecological consciousness.

Izanami and Izanagi's story also has a powerful effect on gender dynamics, with its elements of divine feminism and valorization of male and female roles in creation and destruction processes. Their interplay provides archetypes for masculine and feminine energies which exist harmoniously within Shinto cosmology, making this myth a subject for academic study and discourse.

Ah but wait a second! Within this myth are hidden echoes of ancient shamanic practices; possibly inherited from prehistoric Japan or even other Far Eastern traditions. Thus, Izanami and Izanagi's narrative should not be taken as an isolated event but as part of a larger tapestry woven together from multiple threads with each color contributing to a bigger, more intricate picture.

Enter Japan's Oldest Story Allow me to bring you into an exploration of Japan's oldest story--The Tale of the Bamboo Cutter or as it's traditionally known, "The Tale of Princess Kaguya." Not just another tale; this piece marks the debut of Japanese literature's Monogatari tradition which spans everything from history, romance and adventure all the way to fantasy elements. As its oldest extant narrative it holds an esteemed place among our culture's literary canon and is sure to amaze!

Let's dive in. Imagine you are Okina, an individual living and making their living cutting bamboo in Japan's lush outskirts. While cutting down one radiant stalk after another, an unsuspecting Princess appears; one so small that it can fit perfectly within the palm of your hand! That is right; she lives within the bamboo itself! Okina and his wife Ona decide to adopt Kaguya-hime and call her Kaguya-hime, meaning 'Shining Princess.' Every time Okina cuts bamboo stalks he unearths gold nuggets! Not too shabby for an unassuming woodcutter! Soon enough, they become wealthy enough to provide Kaguya-hime with a life she never could have dreamed of living before. Yet this story goes deeper; exploring existential questions as well as material matters.

But life for radiant Kaguya-hime is far from easy. As she matures into an unparalleled beauty, word of her allure spreads throughout Japan and draws suitors of all kinds--from princes to even the Emperor himself! But Kaguya-hime is no damsel in distress: She sets impossible tasks to these suitors that challenge them like labors of Hercules but with Japanese flair: retrieving Buddha's stone begging bowl or finding jewel-studded branches from mythical islands such as

Horai make these potential lovers scramble to satisfy her demands - sometimes going to great lengths just to win her affections.

Why Does She Do It? Cruelty Or Test? Kaguya-hime's trials aren't random or cruel; they reflect her struggle with identity and place in the world. She understands she doesn't belong here on Earth but rather should return home, leaving behind Earthly life and parents behind in favor of celestial ones--making it all the more heart-wrenching as she wrestles between celestial vs terrestrial forces at play in her heartbreak-inducing dilemma.

As you explore this intricate narrative, themes of loss, love, and human desire emerge. Kaguya-hime's suitors--despite their exalted social positions--are humbled when they fail to fulfill her tasks; not just because their failure echoes Kaguya-hime's internal conflicts; by setting unattainable challenges she subconsciously highlights the gap between her celestial birthplace and Earthly existence which cannot be bridged through money, status or love alone.

5.4 The Tale of the Bamboo Cutter: Japan's Oldest Story

Imagine yourself as Okina, a bamboo cutter living on Japan's idyllic outskirts. While cutting down an radiant bamboo stalk, you encounter a diminutive princess--

small enough for you to fit inside it--into which they adopt her and name her Kaguya-hime, the Shining Princess. Soon thereafter, every time Okina cuts down a bamboo stalk he finds a nugget of gold--something no ordinary woodcutter could hope to encounter! Soon enough they become rich; soon they can afford her life of luxury she imagined in Japan's rural outskirts! But this story delves deeper; its narrative explores existential questions which go far beyond material realities to bring life and emotion--making this film timeless!

But life for Kaguya-hime is far from smooth sailing. As she blossoms into an exceptional beauty, news of her beauty quickly spreads around Japan and beyond-- drawing interest from prospective suitors near and far - princes and even the Emperor himself are attracted by her splendor! But Kaguya-hime is no damsel in distress: She sets impossible tasks for each potential lover that serve as labors of Hercules-style labors of Horai in which retrieving begging bowl of Buddha or retrieving jeweled branches from mythical island Horai make potential lovers scramble about before finding what could possibly make them fall in love!

So why does Kaguya-hime do this? Are her trials cruel or intended as tests? In truth, these trials are more of an expression of her struggle with her identity and place in the world than anything else. You see, Kaguya-hime knows she does not belong on Earth--her true home is on the Moon where she will eventually return, leaving behind all she loves here on Earth including both parents. Her trials thus become manifestations of this inner conflict--ethereal against material; celestial against terrestrial.

Follow this tangled, thrilling narrative and you will encounter themes of loss, love and the complexity of human desire. Kaguya-hime's suitors find themselves humbled when unable to meet Kaguya-hime's tasks; yet these mortal men serve as mirrors to Kaguya-hime's internal struggles: by setting challenges that she knows can never be met she subliminally emphasizes the gap between celestial origins and Earthly existence - one which cannot be bridged through gold or status or even love.

The Tale of the Bamboo Cutter is an emotional rollercoaster, perfectly embodying "Mono no Aware", or the fragility of life. As Kaguya-hime despairs over having to abandon Earthly life and contemplates her transient happiness we're led into reflecting upon fleeting moments that define life; these thoughts leave us reeling with both sadness and admiration at once. However, the narrative manages it so masterfully it leaves us with both sorrowful sadness as well as inspiring wonder.

Epic Bonus 2: Comparative Mythology: Echoes and Reflections

6.1 Common Archetypes Across Different Cultures

Welcome, story lovers! Today we're exploring comparative mythology! But before your eyes glaze over, let me assure you: this topic is far from dull; in fact, it reveals an intricate tapestry woven from different cultures and historical timelines that spans multiple time zones and cultures - Greek myths, Native American folklore or India's Mahabharata all contain archetypes which you may find both familiar and captivating!

What exactly are archetypes, you might ask? Imagine them as the building blocks of storytelling: each myth, legend and folktale you have ever come across contains archetypes as its core elements. Narrative structures form the cornerstones of stories that transcend cultures; that's why so many stories seem similar even though they come from far-flung locales. Are You Seeking Hero Archetypes or Mentor Figures? There is something heroic and transformative about heroes - those stalwart characters on an unending quest for something greater. Known from myths such as Hercules or Rama, or more recently Superman. Plus there are wise old men like Merlin or Gandalf or even native American figure Coyote helping guide our heroes along their transformative journeys.

Archetypal stories also play a central role. Have you noticed how similar King Arthur's search for the Holy Grail and Yoruba mythology's hero's trials are, or their similar struggles as warrior heroes facing mortality - both Mesopotamian Gilgamesh and Greek Achilles come to mind as examples - are striking resemblances. That is no accident; archetypes work their magic beneath disparate cultures to unite them all through archetypes that shimmer beneath the surface but nevertheless unify all cultures through archetypes!

Carl Jung was the pivotal figure in this space, proposing the notion of the collective unconscious: an extensive mental library filled with images, symbols, and archetypes that all humans share. According to Jung's theory of archetypes as deeply-seated parts of human experience - not simply random bits - they form part of our inherited potentials that drive human behavior and represent basic experiences. This groundbreaking idea provided us with an entirely different lens through which to view myths and their pan-cultural lives.

No one could miss the infamous trickster archetype! This character doesn't abide by traditional rules and often causes upheaval or causes mischief to usher in new ideas or opportunities for growth or enlightenment. From Loki in Norse mythology to Anansi from African folklore, tricksters serve a greater purpose: challenging established order in order to bring about growth or illumination. They don't simply cause mischief for no good purpose - rather they act as catalysts of change!

Scholars believe that archetypes may even have evolutionary roots, as some scholars assert their prevalence has evolved through time. Let me explain: over millennia, these archetypes have become embedded into our collective unconscious as survival tools for millennia; for instance, The hero's journey symbolizes humanity's struggle against adversity while teaching us that hardship and struggle are part of life itself - these stories act like survival guides providing instruction on navigating its complexity.

Archetypes serve as the base for myths; however, each culture adds their own twist in terms of interpretation and external form. While their essence remains the same, external manifestations vary considerably and make each myth special while at the same time appealing universally - think of them like stories told across many languages but with unique symbols or characters but ultimately embodying an emotional or spiritual truth shared across cultures; think of each cultural detail being like different colors that form one beautiful mosaic that comes together when taken as a whole.

As we explore various myths, comparing apples with oranges, remember that archetypes are more than literary devices: they represent who we are as individuals and show our interconnection across time and continents; bridges revealing humanity's narrative across history epochs and continents that is worth exploring despite its complexity.

6.2 The Monomyth: The Hero's Journey in World Myth

Hold on tight; Joseph Campbell coined this word "monomyth," an umbrella term for all kinds of myths, legends, and epics from across cultures around the globe that fits snugly together like an elastic waistband. Since its introduction by Campbell in his seminal work "The Hero With a Thousand Faces," monomyths have served as a means to comprehending how disparate cultures may share similar mythologies even while maintaining distinct traditions and landscapes; serving as a kind of mythological Rosetta Stone for helping us all comprehending how global myths often sound similar despite disparate traditions or landscapes differences - such as variations on an everlasting tune!

The concept behind hero tales is marvelously straightforward yet mind-bogglingly expansive: A hero ventures forth from their mundane world into another dimension of wonders, confronts a crisis, triumphs triumphantly and returns home transformed. Their shape can vary greatly--ranging from male to female, young to old, human or godly--while the trials can include everything from slaying dragons, rescuing prisoners, solving uncrackable riddles to confronting internal demons both literally and metaphorically.

Let's pause for a moment and explore two myths in more depth. In Greek mythology, Theseus the young Athenian hero travels to Crete in order to face off against Minotaur, an enormous beast made up of three heads. Unarmed only with Ariadne's magic thread, Jason navigates a treacherous labyrinth, kills Minotaur, and returns home - only to discover that his journey had come at a cost to other parts of himself and those close to him. Now move halfway across the globe to ancient India, where Rama is on a quest to rescue his abducted wife Sita from demon-king Ravana and to return her safely home to her kingdom during Rama's reign. Rama must face many challenges along his journey and receive divine assistance in order to succeed; ultimately he defeats Ravana and returns victorious with Sita safely back in his care - all this while returning the favor by wisely ruling over it all back at home! Each culture, characters and challenges vary, yet at their core lies one monomythic structure waiting patiently behind each of them all:

So why is the Hero's Journey such a widespread idea? One plausible theory echoes our previous discussion on archetypes - it resonates with human experience universally, depicting our struggle against adversity, fears and aspirations in narrative form - offering hope that we too have what it takes to overcome obstacles, with greatness possible if only we dare enter unknown territory! Pretty uplifting stuff?

But let's not get too carried away: the Hero's Journey isn't perfect and is often met with criticism; some scholars point out its Western and patriarchal roots and raise the question whether its application fits all narratives equally or whether certain stories more easily fit its mold than others. All this should provide plenty of intellectual food for thought as we progress further together.

Digging deeper, you'll discover that the Hero's Journey often incorporates specific stages or archetypes--like the Mentor, Threshold Guardian, or Shapeshifter--to make for an engaging narrative experience. Ever wondered why wise old wizards and cunning tricksters keep popping up across cultures? It could be that these figures represent global archetype casting calls that resonate with human instincts and experiences globally; Dumbledore, Gandalf and Yoda all play similar roles: providing guidance and knowledge to our heroes--just like seasoning added into a well-prepared meal!

At least, women can play the hero! While traditional Hero's Journey narratives have often been criticized for being overtly androcentric, let us not forget that powerful women have also trodden this archetypal path - consider Sumerian goddess Inanna who descended into the underworld, faced trials, died, and was reborn - or Mulan from Chinese folklore who defied societal norms to become a war hero and save her nation - both represent female variations on this archetypal narrative that explores women as protagonists while maintaining its core structure but with unique challenges and perspectives brought by being female characters within patriarchal settings - an archetypal journey where women were not represented!

Now, you may be asking: does knowing the details of the Hero's Journey diminish its power to mesmerize us? In fact, understanding its framework increases its magical appeal. Appreciating its structure helps one appreciate all of its rich details--cultural brushstrokes, unexpected turns and depth of character development--and each rendition becomes an intriguing study in both conformity and uniqueness; an echo of an age-old tale told with modern flair.

Reiterating why this concept is essential to comparative mythology, let's highlight its value for comparative mythology: the Hero's Journey serves as an adaptive framework for comprehending essential human narratives across geographic, cultural and temporal borders. By linking seemingly disparate myths together we can reveal universal human searches for meaning, identity and transformation - after all this is one goal of studying mythology: finding those universal threads which connect all humanity together within its vast fabric of human experience.

6.3 Tales of Creation and Destruction: A Global View

Let's switch gears now, and explore something that has long captivated humanity's imagination: creation and destruction myths. You know - those cosmic-scale awe-inspiring narratives which attempt to answer such fundamental questions as: Where did we come from and Where are we headed. Those are what I mean.

Imagine this: every culture has their own version of a creation myth. There's something both humbling and inspiring about that fact; perhaps our questions about life today echo with those raised by ancient Sumerians or Aztec priests from centuries past - an opportunity for bonding with our ancestors!

Let's embark on a brief global tour. First stop: Mesopotamia and "Enuma Elish." Here, the epic depicts Marduk as he battles the primordial sea-dragon Tiamat until she is torn in half by Marduk and becomes the earth and heavens respectively - an elegant metaphor for chaos/order duality found across human cultures and belief systems alike. And to further emphasize our point, Chinese cosmogony also includes references to this theme when Pangu is created as world creation! Seemingly all around?

Native American myths feature stories in which Earth was formed on the back of an animal such as a turtle or another. This "World on the Turtle's Back" narrative not only illustrates animals and Earth's relationship, but it serves as an excellent lesson in interdependence and ecology--both topics we could still learn a great deal from today. Keep an eye out for this concept when studying other traditions; it often pops up unexpectedly!

Hold on tight for an epic Hindu mythological adventure--the dissolution and re-creation of the universe through cycles presided by Brahma, Vishnu, and Shiva--that will take your breath away! What's striking is how this circular perspective contrasts starkly with Abrahamic religions' linear worldview - it's like comparing two circles with profoundly differing philosophical implications; both can produce profound results!

Not to forget Norse mythology either: Ragnarok, an end-of-the-world saga full of epic battles and natural disasters before cosmic reordering occurs, strikes a chord here through its message of renewal after catastrophe: from its ashes arises a new world;

something found across numerous mythologies such as Zoroastrian Frashokereti or Mayan cycles of creation and destruction - comforting, or unnerving? Isn't it comforting- or unnerving- to know that all ends don't really end?

Take a quick break for some expert advice: if all these cross-cultural similarities seem confusing, try drawing out a "mythological mind-map." Starting from an initial concept such as creation and linking it with various mythologies you encounter will help your brain make sense of everything; like seeing constellations for the first time! Everything starts to make more sense.

One intriguing aspect that needs to be mentioned is the dualistic nature of myths. Consider Zoroastrianism where Ahura Mazda, the god of light, engages in constant conflict with Ahriman, the god of darkness; or consider Egypt with Set versus Osiris--brothers representing opposing aspects of creation--tug-of-war which illustrates an almost yin/yang interplay of forces reminiscent of many spiritual systems from Taoism to Neoplatonism that explore these duality--food for thought indeed!

Let's continue our exploration of duality with an African Yoruba myth in which Olorun creates the universe but leaves its completion up to lesser gods such as Obatala. This delegation of creation tasks sounds familiar? It echoes that found in Platonian and Gnostic philosophy's Demiurge where its creator shapes material world creation without necessarily being its ultimate source - an intriguing approach to cosmic craftsmanship!

Let's not forget the Polynesian myths! In Maori tradition, Rangi and Papa - primal parents from Maori traditions - were separated to create space - this event mirrored by physical and emotional separation that resonates across time and space; such an experience must make any theoretical physicist absolutely delighted!

Now let's consider the taboo theme. From mythological tales, such as Pandora's Box or the biblical Apple, forbidden actions have often resulted in chaos or punishment and act as a social glue, providing norms and boundaries. Taboo stories provide valuable lessons about what not to do - the best way of teaching children what to do!

Attention please: to give our discussion some visual stimulation, add an example of an intricate tapestry or mural depicting these many myths; perhaps one which melds cultural elements together into a collage-style work would work perfectly as well - both to provide visual relief while emphasizing interdependency between all our points of discussion.

Creation and destruction myths are more than mere remnants from history; they're living, breathing entities that influence our collective psyche today. They pose questions, spark debates and often provide answers - cosmic puzzles for which humanity has long sought answers through storytelling. So next time you hear one, don't simply sit there listening--involve yourself by engaging, pondering and questioning what it could tell us about our complex human experience! Who knows; it might just hold the key.

Conclusions

So here we are at the conclusion of our journey through mythology! I find the end to be bittersweet; I can't help feeling that we have been part of something bigger and longer-lived; exploring ancient lands, cosmic mysteries, gods and heroes from history's pages who continue to shape culture today; discovering myths are more than mere stories - they represent human thought and culture with its intricate tapestries of dreams, lessons, and aspirations that has guided so much of what we've seen thus far.

Assume nothing: this isn't really the end! Myths are like rivers: they keep flowing, evolving and enriching human civilization. We've only just scratched the surface! There are myriad tales waiting to be explored and interpreted! Whether reading from home or a cozy cafe; whether newbie or experienced mythophile alike--your journey with mythology has only just begun!

Now, I would suggest including an eye-catching mosaic--perhaps featuring iconic symbols from different mythologies, like Thor's hammer, Horus' Eye of Horus, or Japanese Imperial Regalia--to showcase all the different worlds we've visited, while serving as a vivid reminder that stories connect us all together.

Before we wind this chapter down (literally), let's pause to consider why this journey matters. Why should we care about myths from bygone civilizations, you might ask? Because understanding mythology is like unlocking our collective human treasure chest; it provides insights into fears, joys, and aspirations shared across human cultures and provides empathy through reflection of universals of human experience. Let's keep the conversation going - keep exploring, questioning, mythologizing... and let's go mythologizing!

As always, dear reader, I hope our journey together continues indefinitely! May your life be as full and colorful as the myths we've explored together - here's to more incredible adventures through time!

Made in United States
Troutdale, OR
11/16/2023